Get To
be happy

Stories and Secrets to Loving the Sh*t Out Of Life

Ted Larkins

Get To
be happy

Stories and Secrets to Loving the Sh*t Out Of Life

TED LARKINS

Get To
be happy

ISBN: 978-0-9995140-0-9

Printed in the United States of America

© 2017 by Ted Larkins

Cover Design
Bob Cashatt
Pat Torrence
Gabriel Gandzjuk • hellogabriel.com

Interior Design and Layout
Bob Cashatt • RyeChusBytes.com

Website Development
InfoBridge Solutions • infobridgesolutions.com

Editing
Diana Plattner • plaidhatbooks.com

Inquiries should be directed to support@tedlarkins.com.

http://gettoprinciple.com

To my wife, Beth, and my children,
Will and Nia.

We get to do this!

To Mom, Dad, Cole Grace, and Nick
(and all the rest on the other side).

You get to do that!

To my sisters, Kathy and Julie.
There's more to hummingbirds than meets the eye.

I love you.

Contents

Contents continued

"At the end of the day people won't remember what you said or did, they will remember how you made them feel."

—*Maya Angelou*

"Ladies and gentlemen, the story you are about to see is true. The names have been changed to protect the innocent."

—*Dragnet*, 1951

Ladies and gentlemen, the story you are about to read is true. None of the names have been changed to protect the innocent. We're all innocent.

—*Get To Be Happy*, 2017

Foreword

It isn't usual for a book's editor to write the foreword, unless she's a well-known expert on the subject or perhaps some kind of celebrity. I'm neither an expert on gratitude and positive outlooks nor a celebrity of any sort (unless you count the opinions of my dog and two cats, to whom I'm something of a cult hero). But after walking this path with Ted Larkins for months on end, I knew I wanted to write the foreword, and I hoped he'd let me do it, my ordinariness notwithstanding. I felt the book deserved a witness—someone in the front row to stand up and say, *Yep, this guy is for real.* Because when you emerge, humming with positive energy, from the world between these covers, and something upsetting crosses your path, your belief will waver. *Oh, bullshit,* you'll think. *Nobody's really that way. No one can sustain this Get To idea in this kind of traffic, with a collection notice in the glove compartment and the latest bad news on the radio.*

Ted is living proof that it's not only possible, it's worth trying. When you spend time running the three-legged sack race that is the author-editor relationship, you learn a great deal about the other person. The editor, especially, learns about the author. Like most editors, I know how language works. I know how it's used to conceal, spin, inflate, and disguise. It's like my Spidey sense: I know when an author is a well-concealed misogynist or a closet alcoholic, or when she doubts what she preaches, or—at the very least—when the author simply isn't being straight with the reader. Reading in general is one of the few acts that brings another person inside the solitary confinement of your own skull. Editing is reading, magnified.

So I'm here to assure the reader that, yes, this guy is for real, and he's worth your attention—that what you see/read is absolutely what you get: an entertaining author who is upbeat, brimming with enthusiasm, and very much in earnest.

On the face of it, this is a straightforward memoir—Ted was born, stuff happened, he wrote a book. When you get in there, though, you won't find any expected memoir themes, like "how great personal courage (or some other heroic quality) helped me overcome adversity." It's not a rags-to-riches tale, or a redemption narrative, or a coming-of-age story. There's no dramatic arc. In fact, the "stuff that happened" is random, in the way that lives really are. The narrator makes plans, but they often come to nothing. Those that succeed (like learning to play drums in a high-school garage band) sometimes lead to greater things; sometimes they're just small, self-contained joys that play no further role in the story. There are failures, false starts, and near-disasters, as well as moments of joy, but they don't lead anywhere predictable. Hell, they don't really lead anywhere at all, which is sort of the point.

So, what *is* the point? That life is random, except when it isn't. That the only power anyone has over her or his own life is the power to choose a state of gratitude. As Ted points out, when we realize we "get to" do the dishes rather than we "have to" do them, our lives undergo a sea change.

One more thing: Somewhere in here you're going to realize that the "get to" stance comes more naturally to Ted than to most of the rest of us. It's not something he discovered in a cave in Tibet and used to turn his life around. He was born that way. But you'll also find that Ted's knack for "getting to" doesn't disqualify him from sharing the technique, any more than being an Olympic runner disqualifies one from teaching high school track. He's an able guide, and this is territory he knows well.

—Diana Plattner

Preface

You're born, and then you die.
And in between you Get To do this
thing called life!

This book is going to change your life. That's a tall order, I know. But through some light hypnosis and entertaining storytelling, this book is going to re-orient your brain—and you'll become happier in life. Are you ready?

To start, I want to say that I love being a human. The other day, a colleague named Brian came into my office and said, "Hey, I just bought this organic almond butter at the farmer's market. It's got ginger pieces mixed in. It's delicious." He had extra spoons (making the rounds in the office) and handed me one. He opened the jar, and I scooped out a nice large dollop and put it in my mouth. Like peanut butter, but with the distinct almond taste, bits of the almonds crunching in my mouth, along with the tang of the ginger pieces. I closed my eyes and stood savoring that moment. How lucky was I to be having that sensational experience? *Wow.* I smiled, remembering that I was having a Get To moment. I love being a human!

This story illustrates a most basic, yet powerful, aspect of human life: The ability to Get To appreciate, with profound awareness, what is happening to us at any moment. This book charts my journey, living life from this perspective and noticing the miracles that materialized along the way. As you read, you'll start to incorporate this attitude and start experiencing your own miracles.

It's this viewpoint of "getting to" that allows the essence of life to come alive. What I share here with you is not new. The Get To way of living is an age-old understanding handed down through every religion and belief system ever created, but with different names: "Christ consciousness," "being one with Allah," "being here now," "living in the moment," "experiencing God's grace." It's a way of life that monks and sages over millennia have employed to live a peaceful life. It's what current-day, everyday people do to enjoy peace and have a richly fulfilled existence.

I didn't always call it Get To, although I lived that mindset from the time I was a child. The label for what I was experiencing came to me one day when I was talking to my young son, who had just asked me to play with him. I said, "Hang on buddy, I gotta go pee first." As I neared the bathroom it dawned on me, "I don't gotta go pee—I *get to* go pee." In that moment I realized that this "get to" was the fundamental principle by which I'd lived my entire life. It was the "secret," if you will, to my success and happiness. Every breath, taste, sight, smell, touch, every thought and every experience I have, I have because I Get To, and this is how I view life. I also realized, at that moment, that clarifying and identifying it, giving it a name, could help me be more deliberate in entering that state of mind. As I continued to think about it, I realized it could help wake up this way of thinking that is in everyone, and help people live a happier life. I call it the Get To Principle.

There are two aspects of the Get To Principle: First, you Get To do much of what you do, and each thing you Get To do is something many others cannot. This feeling brims with compassion for others and gratitude for what you have. Second, you Get To experience this life in the first place. Right now, as you are reading this book, this moment-to-moment experience that we humans have is miraculous. It's billowing out in front of us every second. Many scientists and spiritual leaders will tell you there is no past or future. There's just one infinite moment happening—right now!

So what is this thing called life? You don't have to come up with an answer, and I certainly won't offer one, but that we Get To do "this" is mind boggling. It makes me smile. Recognizing this, I promise, will make you smile, too!

I am a bartender disguised as a business executive. I say bartender because some of the most formative years of my life were lived behind the bar, whether at the MGM Casino in Reno, the Sheraton Hotel in San Diego, the swanky Tribeca restaurant in Beverly Hills, or the Wild West Club in Osaka, Japan. Who I am and many of my views on life have been shaped by those experiences. I'm not rich, although—as you'll read—compared to Stanley in India, I'm a bazillionaire. And as you'll see, like everyone else, I have had my many ups and downs, joys and sorrows in life. But using the Get To Principle has brought me to a point of sincere bliss and joy much of the time. Even when things suck, I Get To live through them, too. It's very liberating.

I'm writing this book because I want to share this idea and help bring peace to the world. Okay, maybe creating world peace is a little exaggerated. Although it's true that I love helping people and I especially love sharing the Get To way of life, I'm not all saintly with grandiose visions of changing the world. I am not a guru. In fact, I'm a non-guru—the factors that have me sitting here typing away are a bit more mundane.

First: I always wanted to write something a little more in-depth than *The Babysitter's Business Guide* that I self-published 30 years ago.

Second: I'm commuting to work four hours a day on the train (yes, in Los Angeles where it's almost sacrilegious not to sit in traffic), so I thought I'd put my time to good use.

Third: I recently listened to the audio version of Elizabeth Gilbert's book, *Big Magic*, which is specifically about creativity, Liz's personal journey (yeah, my pal Liz, whom I've never met), and her advice on writing, especially after her hit novel *Eat, Pray, Love*. She talks about how creativity is in everyone, but most of us never act on it. She wrote, "On bad days when I felt no inspiration at all, I would set the kitchen timer for 30 minutes and I would make myself sit there and scribble something, anything." She also advised, "Whether you think you're brilliant, or you think you're a loser, just make whatever you need to make and toss it out there."

So I've come to realize the following: (A) I've always wanted to write; (B) although I don't think I'm a complete loser, I've been afraid to take action; and (C) I've certainly got 30 minutes a day that I can dedicate to sharing my vision. So here I am on the train, writing this book: Toss!

• • • •

The quotes at the beginning of each chapter were either in-spired by or came directly from several journals I kept over the last 35 years. Some came from dozens of cassette-tape "letters" I sent to my dad during my travels through Asia in the 1990s. (I found them in the back of a drawer when going through the things in his house after he died in 2010.) Others are credited to someone specific.

At the end of each chapter I offer practical exercises using the Get To Principle and the *"Get To—Smile—Do it!"* mantra I'll introduce in the next chapter. As I said earlier, the Get To way of thinking is in everyone, and the exercises will help awaken that capacity in you. They will change your life by bringing you to great appreciation for the moments you're living in. They are there for those who want to do them, and to be skipped by those who don't. My advice is to jump—embrace the fear (or whatever else you may feel) and do them anyway. If you make the exercises part of your life, you'll see small, magical results as they germinate, and you'll understand why I'm urging you to take up these habits. You'll want to develop some of your own, as well. The key is in noticing the small transformations, which snowball into large transformations.

Also, as you'll see, I suggest doing some of the exercises regularly for 30 days. I don't believe in the "30 days to make a habit" theory, per se. You really just have to decide to do something (or not), and then you'll do it until you decide to do something different. However, if you can commit to something for 30 days, you'll know you're on the right track to making a difference in your life.

Here's an example of how the Get To Principle works. The other day I woke up at 1 a.m. with a stomachache. I knew what it meant: both of my young kids had spent the previous several days puking their guts out, and now it was my turn. By 2 a.m., I was on the bathroom floor with a bucket next to me. I will spare you the details on that. When I emerged at 4 a.m., my wife asked how I was (she hadn't been able to sleep through the noise), and I grinned and said, "Well, I got to do that." I was in awe of the human body, for one thing, and for another, as opposed to spending two hours on the floor of a cold mud hut, I have a heated toilet seat and was about to crawl into a bed with the softest of down comforters. In short, I felt compassion for those who are living with almost nothing, and I was grateful for what I have and in awe of the magic of life, including the maladies of the body. That's the Get To journey—welcome aboard!

1. Get To Know the Get To Principle

Change "I gotta do the dishes" to "I Get To do the dishes," and your life transforms.

Applying the Get To Principle to your life is simple: At any given moment, in any given circumstance, facing any given task, you say to yourself (or out loud), "I Get To do this." You smile, then you do what you were going to do. *Get To—Smile—Do it! Get To—Smile—Do it!* Using this mantra works as a mechanism for shifting your attitude and relating to the world differently.

In almost every situation in my life, I use *Get To—Smile—Do it!* to settle my mind and change my perspective. The famous psychologist William James wrote: "The greatest discovery of my generation is that man can alter his life simply by altering his attitude of mind." When you say I Get To do something, the mind automatically stops regretting the past or worrying about the future because you move from the victim of "I have to" to the power of "I get to"—and in that moment, your mind becomes still. Next, in that silence, when you smile, your brain reacts positively. In his article "There's Magic in Your Smile," Ronald E. Riggio, PhD, states: "Each time you smile you throw a little feel-good party in your brain. The act of smiling activates neural messaging that benefits your health and happiness." The Buddhist monk and peace activist Thich Nhat Hanh says, "Sometimes your joy is the source of your smile, but sometimes your smile can be the source of your joy." And then, from that space of stillness where you've created joy, when you do whatever you were going to do, there is a sense of freedom and of being in charge of how you are experiencing what is happening in life.

This practice can produce amazing results—like ease and happiness—in both the short term and the long term, and in both negative and positive situations. In really brutal life transitions, it might not exactly be "happiness," but the Get To Principle frames things with wisdom and calm. It allows you to accept with gratitude what life presents to you in every moment, regardless of the "flavor" of that particular moment.

With the death of my daughter, I got to experience the sorrow and joy that comes with accepting the inevitable coming and going of life.

When I held my dying friend, as he took his last breath, I got to be with grace in a choice to end a painful existence.

During more than 3 million miles of flying in airplanes around the world, when most people I sat next to were complaining about all the traveling, I kept thinking, "I get to hurtle through the sky at 500 miles an hour reading a book, or watching movies, or just—being. How great is this?" The reality is, when you think about it at all, we're on a ball hurling through space at 67,000 miles per hour. Michael Singer, in his book *The Untethered Soul*, says it best: "You're floating in empty space in a universe that goes on forever. If you have to be here, at least be happy and enjoy the experience."

Several months ago an executive in the company I work for came in from the head office to chat. He had recently been promoted to oversee the expansion of one of the divisions of the company. There would be several new teams under him, so it was a big deal at our publicly traded company. We were chatting and he was talking about all the challenges facing him. He was worried and concerned at the foreseeable burden—the workload. At some point I said, "But the challenges are what make it so exciting. *You get to do this.*" He paused a moment, and then smiled and said, "Oh my God, you're right. I *get to do* this. It *is* exciting, and under all the thoughts about how tough it's going to be, I'm actually very excited!" He said it again, "Wow, I get to do this!" He smiled. I love watching that shift from *have to*, to *get to*.

As I said earlier, there are two outcomes of the Get To Principle. First is a feeling of intense appreciation for your life because others can't do or have something that you can; second is a deep understanding that life itself is a miracle. The first one is powerful in itself. Those of us in the industrialized first-world countries have luxuries only dreamed of by many people on the planet. It's a shift in viewpoint that is filled with gratitude for our personal reality, and compassion for others with less than we have.

The second outcome is even more powerful when it's fully experienced. In fact, I think that full understanding of the Get To Principle could be considered a form of enlightenment. I obviously don't fully understand the Get To Principle myself, because I'm far from enlightened, but sometimes when I use the *Get To—Smile—Do it!* mantra, I become so giddy with joy for this experience of life that I feel like I'm about to pop over the edge into that vast oneness with everything. (I'll explain that last sentence in a coming chapter about a "spiritual awakening" I had.) Many of us seem to be searching for more and more to occupy our minds, more experiences to bring us joy and happiness. But you don't need to climb Mt. Everest to have an incredible experience. Simply being fully aware of the present moment can make any "grand experience" pale in comparison and blow your mind.

I can't wait to see what adventures people have with this, where they take it. I would love a few monks to take it on as a mantra, repeating "I get to do this, I get to do this, I get to do this" over and over for a few months, and see if they have an awakening of some sort—maybe have instantaneous levitation sessions? Sitting quietly hour after hour, year after year imagining the sound of one hand clapping is a great exercise, but why not use "I get to do this"?

Practice

Repeat the *Get To—Smile—Do it!* exercise at least ten times a day for 30 days. (For perspective, I say *Get To—Smile—Do it!* at least 50 times a day. It's a habit. At first, I had to catch myself saying "I have to" or "I gotta" and change my attitude to "I get to" instead. Now saying "I get to do this" is a *way* of life. The smile has become both automatic and genuine.) Decide to change your habit of saying "I have to" and instead say, "I get to!" You can put a rubber band on your wrist and snap it whenever you catch yourself feeling like "you gotta," if that helps. You can track every time you remember to "get to" do things on a notecard, or even keep a journal in which you examine how you felt both before and after using the Get To Principle. In that 30 days, the joy will increase in your life, the Get To Principle will become part of your outlook, and you will become happy and wise—or at least, happier and wiser. Yep, that's a promise.

Get To—Smile—Practice.

2. Get To Grow Up

"I'm lucky to know that I'm lucky to be having this experience called life."
Think about that until you smile.

I believe we define ourselves slowly by the infinite experiences we have daily and by our responses to them. In addition, most people have several major life-changing experiences that alter their viewpoints dramatically. I, for one, have had my share. So allow me, in the coming chapters, to share a bit of who I am, relaying a few of the various experiences that have made up my life through the Get To way of being.

My life beginnings were pretty mundane. I was born into a middle-class family in Chicago in 1962, and in 1969, when I was seven years old, my family moved to Columbus, Ohio, where I grew up. Yep, nice and mundane.

It was a pretty straightforward childhood. We were a four-kid family, each basically two years apart. Kathy was the oldest, followed by my brother, Rick. I was number three, and then came Julie. Mom, after getting us past diapers, was a schoolteacher, and Dad, after years selling steel in Chicago (yep, selling steel), started a janitorial service, cleaning buildings around Columbus. Mom's dad was a politician, serving as Ohio's secretary of state for nearly 30 years. Dad's dad was the athletic director of Ohio State University. Mom and Dad were a match made in heaven. Or not. We'll see how that turns out shortly.

I was about as average as they come. I just wanted to be liked by the cool kids, and not get beat up by the bullies. But the cool kids wouldn't have me and I spent a lot of time running away from other kids throwing mud balls at me. One warm spring afternoon walking home from school, when I was eight years old, a group of kids led by a girl named Amy chased me and knocked me down. I had made it to my driveway before they caught me—heck, I'd almost made it to the house. Amy got on top of me, pinning my arms with her knees as she sat on my chest laughing. I don't remember why they were after me but I was crying, which made her, and the four or five other kids standing around her, laugh harder. In that moment, lying there looking up at her, with the smell of the warm blacktop in my nose and the crisp blue sky above, I decided that I would never let that happen again. I vowed to be strong, get a black belt in karate, and come get my revenge. *Not. I* stuffed it down, cried myself to sleep, and am a wimp to this day. Amy and I would become friends in later years, and when I asked about it one day, she didn't remember that incident, just the times we ate peanut-butter-and-marshmallow sandwiches together.

In 1974, at the ripe old age of 12, I did what many kids did back then—I delivered newspapers, something I continued for many years. My paper route was a big deal and provided spending money for my various activities in life, like buying second-hand minibikes and go-carts (and later, pot—but that's a story for another chapter). Every day after school, on Saturday afternoon and early Sunday morning, I would take the bundle of 100 or so newspapers that a truck dropped in front of my house, sit in the garage, undo the metal wire holding them together, then roll each one up and put a rubber band around it. I dreaded the days when there were inserts—separate pages of ads that I would "insert" into each newspaper before rubber-banding them. If it was raining or snowing (the chances of either were pretty good in Columbus), I got to put them in plastic bags. In the early years I would put the wrapped newspapers in my red wagon, then later in baskets on the sides of my Solex or Moped, and finally, at 15 with my temporary driver's permit, in the open trunk of my car.

I'd park whichever vehicle I had halfway up the street, take a shoulder bag of papers, and walk up one side of the street and back down the other dropping a newspaper on the front porch of all of the houses that had a subscription—most did. Then I'd move the vehicle to the next street and start over. Did I mention that it was often raining or snowing? No matter what, I was out there. Just a Midwestern boy in a Norman Rockwell painting, cheerfully delivering his papers.

One bitter Sunday morning at 7 a.m., sometime just before Christmas 1974 and after a night of heavy snow, I went out to do my route. I had been out for an hour and was exhausted tramping through the snow to each of the porches. My hands, feet, and face were numb. My body was numb. As I returned to my wagon after delivering a paper, I noticed a soft-looking snow bank and I decided to take a rest. I was so cold, and the soft snow looked so inviting, I sat down, leaned over—and fell asleep.

I awoke in my Dad's arms in the kitchen in front of the oven, its door pulled open, the temperature on "high." Apparently, Dad had been awakened by a phone call from a client whose building's water pipes had burst and who needed Dad to get over there. On the way, Dad passed by my wagon. At first, in his rush, he kept driving. But be it luck, fate, or angels, he decided to turn around to see how I was doing—and found me in the snow bank, blue. They say that later in life you can never really thank your parents enough for what they did for you. I'll say. I wonder what Norman Rockwell would have made of my father's expression at that moment, or as I woke up in his arms in front of the open oven? Some people turn their noses up at his accessible compositions, but say what you will, he was a master at capturing expressions.

As a kid I also used to vacuum and mop floors at night and on weekends with Dad for extra money. When I turned 16 I quit my paper route and started to go clean buildings by myself. Scrubbing toilets, emptying ashtrays, and looking at the *Playboy* magazines in the men's restrooms at night—a 16-year-old boy's dream.

I would also take crews to clean warehouses and do other jobs. Although I didn't realize it, I learned a lot of the Get To Principle during this time. Many of the people cleaning buildings at night were doing a second job to pay for school, or simply to pay rent. Others were on welfare or out on parole, or just were uneducated and couldn't get another job. White, black, women, men—all were in the same position.

At first I was the "rich" white kid, the owner's son who'd show up at the building to inspect their work. I soon figured out that if I wanted their respect I had to get dirty—and I did. We'd power-scrub a floor, clean out smelly trash cans, or wash grimy windows, sometimes outdoors on oppressively hot Columbus summer nights. We'd take a break and I'd order pizza "on the company," and sit and smoke cigarettes and drink Coca-Cola. I made some great friends and realized that the only difference between me and anyone else was simply what I thought it was. We were all just human beings having our individual experiences, none of us better or worse than any other. We were all just trying to be happy. What great lessons in life.

One of the guys, Melvin, played pool. I was pretty good, so we talked a lot about it. One day he invited me to his local pool hall in downtown Columbus for a billiards tournament. *Sure*, I thought, *why not?* So on the following Friday night, my friend David and I drove down to one of the seedier parts of town, did a one-hit of pot in the parking lot, and walked into the bar.

You know those western movies and the scene where a guy walks through the swinging saloon doors, the piano falls silent, and the barkeep stops pouring a drink? Then everyone turns and stares at the stranger through the haze of smoke, and you hear the whistle from *The Good, the Bad and the Ugly?* That was us: 1978, two white boys entering an all-black bar. For a moment I thought, *Oh shit, bad move coming in here.* My heart was pounding, I couldn't swallow, and just as we were about to leave a voice called out from the back, "Teddy boy, my man, you made it!" and Melvin came up, big white-toothed smile, and gave me a huge hug. The piano started up, the conversations came back alive, and the hustle and bustle at the bar resumed. (There wasn't a piano, I just wrote that for effect. It was probably Kool and the Gang on the juke box.) Melvin introduced us around. Men and women alike looked me up and down and said, "Boy, any friend of Melvin's is a friend of ours!" We drank beer and smoked cigarettes, laughed and shot pool. And I won first place and got a trophy.

Practice

We all did some crazy things as kids, even if it was just playing hooky from school, or taking a drag from a cigarette, or sneaking a beer in a movie. We passed notes in class behind the teacher's back, or snuck into our parents' or a sibling's room and, heart pounding, looked through their drawers. How about an unapproved joy ride in your parents' car? Remember a time you did some radical thing when you were younger.

Get To—Smile—Relive that moment!

Soooo sweet.

Boy Scout Ted, Columbus, 1970.

Larkins family
circa 1967, Chicago.

Dad, a Marine, with his dad,
Richard C. Larkins, 1957.

My mother's father, Ted Brown,
meeting President Gerald Ford.

3. Get To Parents

Our parents were doing the best they could based on what they were taught by their parents, who were doing the best they could based on what they were taught by their parents, and on and on. So give them all a break, and make the change you want in the world starting now.

In 1974, Dad needed a secretary for his office at the house. My ever-generous mom introduced him to her good friend Bekki. Bekki was ten years younger and, to my father, she was hot. In talks with Dad later in life, he said Mom had quit having sex with him (although there's always two sides to that coin), and that Bekki was . . . well as I said, hot, and they fell in love. At the time, I didn't know what was going on, and Mom and Dad pretended everything was fine. Even with the hushed conversations in their bedroom, I thought they were the perfect couple, and we, the perfect family. Over the next several years, as Dad started sleeping on the couch "because of his back" or not coming home at night "because of work," I still thought everything was fine.

But then came the day when we loaded up the '75 Ford station wagon for our annual one-week trip to visit my grandmother at her trailer home in Ft. Myers, Florida. Mom was at the wheel and Dad was in the house, staying home "to attend business." Mom started the car and I was seated in the fold-up bench seat that looked out the back window. (I loved that seat—as you passed truckers on the freeway, if you pulled down on an imaginary rope hanging in midair, you could get them to blow their horn!) The car was a mayhem of us kids getting settled in, filled with blankets and pillows (and probably a pet hamster), coolers and brown paper bags with food. It had a canvas luggage carrier strapped to the top, securely loaded for the 24-hour drive. At the last moment, as we started to back out of the drive- way, Dad came running out with a small white suitcase and jumped in the front passenger seat. I turned around and we all yelled, "Yeah, Daddy's coming!" And then I saw the cold, silent frown on Mom's face in the rearview mirror. That's when I knew it in my heart. The day we got back from Florida, Dad moved out.

By 1978 Mom divorced him, and she was devastated. I just ignored it all. I was a teenager with other priorities (getting high and getting laid), so didn't have much compassion or attention for Mom. One cool fall night, I was walking toward my friend's house for band rehearsal (you'll meet KAX shortly). I was several blocks away and saw this sobbing person, a woman, coming from the other way. "Man," I thought, "that person is a wreck." As we passed on opposite sides of the street I realized it was Mom. She looked at me in anguish and said, "Teddy, I'm sorry you're seeing me like this. Please forget you're seeing it." Really, it was like a horror movie and a crazy woman was saying, *I'm hideous, look away, look away!* I did look away. I continued walking, smoked a joint, and played the drums, though with much less vigor than normal.

Later in life I apologized to Mom for ignoring her and not showing her any compassion, but she was cool. "Ted," she said, "you were doing the best you could. You move on."

After Dad left, she taught school, managed a candle store, and worked at the Dublin Public Library. In 1989 she was diagnosed with breast cancer and was told she had to have a mastectomy on one of her breasts. She said, "If I'm going to do it, I'm going to get them both removed and rebuilt better." The insurance company would only pay for one removal, and not for the reconstruction, either. It was just not done at the time. But Mom was a pioneer. She fought, and in the days before computers, wrote hundreds of letters protesting her right to insurance for a double mastectomy and reconstruction.

And she *won*. She was so proud of them. It's weird, I know, but she was so proud of her boobs that she would show off her profile when I visited. "Mom, really? Do I have to look?" "Teddy," she said (even though I was 30), "it's given me a new lease on life." After that she learned to ballroom dance and became a dance instructor at the famous (in Columbus, anyway) Jimmy Rawlins Dance Studio. Even with her years of suffering (losing your husband to your best friend was the ultimate dagger to the heart in her world), she was always supportive of whatever us kids wanted to do. Through it all, she never wavered in her dedication to pull out of her funk and live a great life. We laughed a lot and she always helped me through tough times, compassionately listening and accepting whatever crazy-ass adventure I was into next. She made several trips to visit me on the West Coast and came to see me when I was living in Japan, and we traveled a lot together, including a trip through Europe and a cruise through the Greek islands. She was awesome.

On an early Friday afternoon, December 21, 2012, to be exact, I was sitting at my desk in my living room, on the phone with a client, when I saw Kathy calling in on the screen. I let it go to voice mail. She called again ten minutes later. I ignored it. Soon after I ended my client call and was doing a follow-up email, I noticed a "Voice Mail [2] messages" notice on my phone. *Oh shit, I forgot, Kathy called.* I dialed my voice mail and listened.

Message one, 1:05 p.m. "Ted, Mom's had some kind of seizure. I just got to her house as they put her in the ambulance. The guys wouldn't let me ride with her, but said she'll be fine. I'm following in the car to the Dublin hospital. Call me. Love you."

Message two, 1:15 p.m. "Hey there. I just got to the hospital. Julie's here. They've got her in the back. It's strange, they brought us into some side waiting room. The doctor said they're working on her and he'll report back. It's worse than I thought. Anyway, call me back. Love you."

I looked at the clock, now showing 1:30. I called Kathy: "Hey Kath, got your voice mail, how's Mom?"

Kathy said in a quiet voice, "She's had what looks like a heart attack. They're in the back working on her." She got quieter and said, "Ted, it's not looking good."

"What do you mean it's not looking good? What does that mean? Kathy? Hello?" I heard shuffling as someone came into the room. Kathy whispered, "Oh, God, a priest just came in."

"*What?* Kathy, what's happening?" I asked, panicked. I heard muffled talking. Then someone crying. "*Kathy!*" I yelled. "Kathy, what—is—*happening?*"

Silence for a beat, and then, "Ted, Mom's gone."

"No, no, no, *no, no!*" I was screaming, and then sobbing, and I couldn't stop—"No, no, no!"—and Kathy hung up on me.

I went to the couch and lay down and wailed. Kind of like you see on the news of funerals in the Middle East. That was me. (On later reflection I would feel a new respect for other cultures' grieving processes.) I wasn't crying, I was wailing.

At some point Beth drove up and came running in. "Ted, what's going on, I could hear you down the street—while driving in the car! The kids are outside afraid to come in."

I took a deep breath and slowly looked up and then said, "Mom's dead."

The kids (ages eight and five) peered around the doorway, slowly, looking at me. I smiled and said, "It's okay you guys, Daddy's sad and is letting it out. I could use a hug." Tentative at first, they came and hugged me and I told them that grandma had died.

● ● ● ●

As you might imagine, Dad's experience of their divorce was vastly different from Mom's. In 1978, while Mom was experiencing the slow-motion train wreck of her life, Dad was getting laid and was in love. He and Bekki did everything together. He got an office space and she became vice president of the cleaning business. Over the next 25 years they went to work together, had lunch together, went home together. This was a total Get To life for him. They grew the business to 85 part-time employees (me being one) and a modest yearly $1 million in revenue. As the owner of a small business, Dad never made money, but he always had some. Funny how that works. You want to know how close Bekki and Dad were? Dad died of cancer mixed with a heart attack in 2010. Bekki, only 66 years old, died of an until-then-undiagnosed case of emphysema less than three months later. Stunning. How she created that I'll never know, but she wasn't going to live without Dad and got the hell out of Dodge. That is getting to do life on your own terms!

I spent the last week of Dad's life with him. Back in February, I'd come to visit from our home in California. He was sick with melanoma, which had kept coming and going over a number of years. He was also a big 330 pounds and had the diseases that come with that. But he was okay.

As I was leaving, I said, "You've got years left."

He said, "I just want to make it to my birthday in April."

I laughed at that with him as I walked out the door. We talked most days and he seemed good.

Kathy called, however, on Saturday, March 27, and said, "I know you're going on another trip to Japan next week, but you might want to come see Dad before you go."

I said, "He's fine, I talked to him yesterday."

"Ted, "she said, "he's not so fine." Kathy was older by five years, and like with E.F. Hutton, when she spoke, I listened.

I caught a plane to Columbus the next morning.

For the following week, I sat on his bed with him and talked about life and all we had been through. We had gone on several golfing trips, including one to Pebble Beach and another when we met in Hawaii to play. Neither of us were good, but we loved being on the golf course together.

Another time, in 2003, I bought tickets ($800 each on eBay!) for the College Football Championship game in Tempe, Arizona. Ohio State was playing the University of Miami for the title—and we won! When I say "we," I mean Ohio State, of course. As I've mentioned, Dad's dad, my grandfather, was Richard C. Larkins, athletic director of Ohio State from 1947 to 1970. He hired the famous (infamous?) Woody Hayes and is credited for making the Ohio State University athletic program the powerhouse that it is today. Anyway, I got to take Dad to that game, and it was fantastic.

In 2007 I took $10,000 out of my IRA account and flew both of us, business class, to Japan to visit Tokyo and Osaka for a week. Dad had always wanted to fly on a 747, and I thought that was the least I could give back to him for the life he had given me. Beth, my wife (whom you'll meet later), didn't like my taking savings for a vacation with Dad (she was still mad about the football tickets), but it wasn't a question in my mind. I knew it would be a true Get To experience—and it made for precious time when we got to talk about the trip during that week on his bed together.

He also wanted me to find my brother Rick, who had not seen Dad in more than five years. We knew Rick lived somewhere near Columbus, but he never showed up to any family gatherings. Kathy had a phone number that went to an anonymous-sounding voice mail, so she would leave messages for him there, and at an email address she'd found, but he never replied and we never knew if he got the messages. So I sent emails, and left voice mails saying that Dad was dying and wanted to see his son one last time. I used an online detective, called old girlfriends of his, and did what I could to get in touch with him. Dad and I got to do that together, and we laughed a lot.

At one point I said, "Rick's a bastard for abandoning you and Mom."

Dad smiled and said, "It is what it is. He, like you, is doing the best he can. And I love you all the same." That is such a Get To way of thinking, which Dad had more and more as he got older. He was happy.

On Friday, after nearly a week together, I told him, hesitantly, that I was going to go, as planned, to Japan. He of course said, "Get out of here. I'll be fine." But he was frail, with the chemo treatments taking their toll.

As I was leaving I sat on the side of the bed and took his hand and said, "I love you Dad." And then, without thinking, I kept going. "This may be the last time I see you in this life and I want to tell you what an honor it's been to be your son. I'm so lucky for this life I have and it's because of you." I cried, holding in the sobs that would come later, and went on for a few minutes. At some point I asked him to give me a sign from the other side.

He smiled. He never really cried but there were tears, and he said, "Are you done yet? Now go on, no one's dying."

I hugged him hard and headed to the airport. The sobs came as soon as I got in the car.

I landed in Tokyo on Monday afternoon and went straight to a dinner with some coworkers and Linda and Shannon Lee. Linda is Bruce Lee's widow, and Shannon is his daughter. I had met the Lees several years earlier, when my company was developing Bruce Lee products for sale in Japan. We had flown the Lees in for a Bruce Lee touring-memorabilia exhibition we'd set up in Tokyo that week.

We were sitting at the restaurant eating sushi and drinking sake when my phone rang. It was Kathy's number on the screen. I didn't think much of it, and when with clients, I usually don't answer the phone. Still, this time I excused myself and answered. "Hey Kath, what's up?"

A pause, and then she said, "Dad died in his sleep last night."

I gulped, tears welling up in my eyes, and ran out outside. I sat there on a curb in a quiet Tokyo alley, with the bright neon lights all around, and cried with Kathy. (I had said my peace with Dad, so no wailing!) I told her that I would catch the next plane home, and then I went back into the restaurant. I looked at my Japanese friends and then spontaneously looked at Shannon and said, "Please come outside real quick, I need help." A bit confused, she hesitated, but followed me.

Back out in the cool night air I looked at her and said, "Better than anyone, I know you can relate. My dad just died." She gave me a great hug of love while I cried on her shoulder.

I flew home the next day. There was no funeral or service or anything. Dad had told us to do nothing. Kathy, Julie, and I went to the funeral home, and I got to kiss his cold, bald head. I looked at him lying there, and through my tears, I smiled. Life! He had died on April 5, 2010—his 75th birthday.

● ● ● ●

I'm lucky. If you're reading this book, most likely you're lucky, too. Or blessed, or whatever you want to call it. On this planet, 23,347 people died of starvation today. I just Googled it. It's hard to imagine even a single day's suffering in the events that lead to that number. Millions of people lack access to food and fresh water. Millions more live in war-torn areas with no homes and truly no hope. All around you, people are grieving the loss of loved ones at this very moment. Opening ourselves to this universal suffering won't make our deepest losses less painful. But it can give us perspective on our smaller troubles.

Feeling some of the pain of the world can also have a surprising effect. If you breathe deeply and sit quietly with all that suffering, eventually something wells up inside you—and it's not despair, as you might think. It's compassion. That compassion for the world spreads to yourself, and being the receiver of that much compassion lifts you up, strengthens you, makes you grateful for everything you get to experience—even the really big, painful things. And it puts the little things in their place. For me, most "suffering" is when my toast burns, or my train is delayed, or there is heavy traffic and I'm late to dinner at a nice restaurant. Are you kidding me? Please.

Despite all this talk about suffering, I'm not a dark person, as you may have already gathered. My ability to roll with whatever life has to offer, be it a joy or a misery, is partly a result of life experience—but I'd be wrong not to admit I have a knack for it. How much of that ability was inborn, and how much was absorbed from my mother's beautiful example? What if I'd been born to a heroin-addicted mother in a tenement slum—would I be writing this now, and telling you how the Get To Principle can change your life? Or would I be lying dead somewhere with a needle in my arm? I can't answer that. All I can do is be profoundly grateful for every life experience, and for the ability to be grateful.

After the initial shock and grieving over our mother's death, my sisters and I grew to appreciate the way she got to leave this life. At 78, we could tell the dementia was setting slowly in; it wasn't going to get any better. She'd had a massive heart attack and died within minutes. We were able to look at each other and smile. A good life, a good exit. There's nothing wrong with that. We can miss her presence and still get to love how she died. (By the way, December 21, 2012, is the day the Mayan calendar said the world would end. My wife's grandmother and my best friend Pat's mom also died that day. I guess, in a sense, the Mayans got it right.)

With my dad's death, as I mentioned, I got to feel sorrow, love, and—yes—joy as I observed him lying there in the casket. The whole journey, including my 47 years alive with him, had been filled with beautiful moments. The news of his death, which I got on the phone at that restaurant in Tokyo, was delivered by a sister whom I loved, and who loved me. The hug Shannon gave me as I wept outside the restaurant in Tokyo— that was one of the best hugs of my life. The Delta agent who told me there would be a $700 charge to change my flight plans, and who listened as I cried and told her my father had just died, decided to change my flight for free. I love humanity and compassion! And the signs I asked Dad for? Just ask my sisters about hummingbirds.

Five years later, on July 3, 2015, we took his ashes up in a small plane and released them over the Ohio State Stadium. You can see it on YouTube (search for "An Ohio State Buckeye farewell" on YouTube). Yeah, we got to do that!

You could put this book down right now and go help the world. That would be cool. But you don't have to. You don't have to be Gandhi or Mother Teresa. You can, and some will, do great work for the planet and those living on it, whether it's by being like Bill Gates and giving a boatload of money to charities or by doing some local volunteer work. Or you can simply choose to be happy and smile at strangers. That act in itself is giving back to the world in a powerful way. You get to do that, and it's perfect.

We all get to acknowledge the suffering around the world, even our own. With that acknowledgement, there is a natural tendency to give back to the world, to want to help. With the Get To Principle at work in your life, you will begin giving back naturally—because when you realize you get to when others can't, compassion will flow from you and the planet will change.

Practice

I got lucky with Dad and was able to say goodbye. I feel so blessed to have had that opportunity. With Mom, well, we chatted on the phone two days before she died. General stuff, while I was waiting for my friend Ajay to show up for lunch at a restaurant in L.A. When I saw him come in the door I said to Mom, "Oh, gotta run, love you," and hung up. Not bad. If I'd known that would be the last time I'd talk to her I might have been more present. Now, as best as possible, I say to my wife and kids whenever we part, "I love you," and spend a few seconds with appreciation of them. If your parents are living, call them and say, "I love you." Be quiet in the moment with them. If they have passed on, do this exercise in your mind. Do the same thing, as often as possible with everyone.

Get To—Smile—Say "I love you."

Dad and Bekki.

Mom and Dad,
the perfect couple.

Mom and her kids, 1983.

Ted Brown, Secretary of State
inauguration, 1972. I'm far right.

4. Get To High School

This is life. No second chances.
No do-overs. We get to smile or frown.
We get to decide how we are in any
given moment in time.

High school was a blur of fun, and I graduated, which was a bit of a miracle. I was the drum major in the marching band, big tall hat, baton, and all. I would often be out there, marching down the field—stoned and smiling. We were one of those cool high school marching bands where many people stayed in the stands during halftime to watch. Every Friday, in front of hundreds of high school football fans, I was out on the field leading the band, throwing the baton in the air and catching it. One time, I threw it really high, and 30 yards the wrong way on the field— I waved and watched it hit the ground. Everyone cheered. As anyone who has been in a high school marching band will attest, it's no cakewalk. There are many early morning rehearsals of the music, and just as many after-school rehearsals marching on the football field. In Ohio, the football season runs into winter and it gets really cold and twirling a frozen metal baton is no easy feat. The tuba players had it worst, carrying those big heavy pieces of metal, keeping those metal mouthpieces warm. Ouch! But we did it, as all bands do, and it was great.

At 15 I started a rock band called KAX with three other friends. I was the drummer. The singer had a brother with a Southern accent, and "kax" was how he pronounced "cock." I'm not proud of that one, but at 15 that's what you get. We spray-painted KAX in big yellow letters on the trunk of my brown, '72 Pinto. We thought we were pretty cool. On New Year's Day 1978 I used a hacksaw to cut the top off—it was a sweet ride. Anyway, I used my newspaper-route money to buy a double bass, 13-piece, clear-blue Ludwig drum set, as I was hoping to be like Neil Peart of Rush when I grew up. I would put the Rush album *2112* on the record player and pound away hour after hour down in the basement. It vibrated the dishes off the table and you could hear it out on the street. How did my parents stand it? They got to experience that, and I certainly apply the Get To Principle here as well: I have immense compassion for what they must have put up with, and great appreciation that I had a killer drum kit to play.

We were loud and not very good. AC/DC, Led Zeppelin, the Stones, the Ramones, Lynyrd Skynyrd, Aerosmith, Deep Purple, ZZ Top. We played bars on the Ohio State campus, dark dank places that smelled of stale beer—a smell I loved then but would come to despise later in life. We packed our cars with speakers, drums, and guitars, parked in back alleys and carried our shit into the dimly lit rooms and set up on tiny stages. Then we rocked out for two 45-minute sets. Mostly it was our friends (my girlfriend, Jamie, was always there) and my family and a couple of winos off the street. We had an agent (he actually wore a tie) who booked us at high school proms around Ohio. Our slow song at those gigs was "Stairway to Heaven." God I wish I had some video footage of us playing for those kids, not much younger than us, slow dancing until we got to the fast part and then looking at us and saying, "What the fuck?" It was so fun. We were drinking, getting high, smoking cigarettes by the pack. And playing music. What I couldn't know at the time was that learning to play the drums would create, years later, a life-changing opportunity in Japan.

I've mentioned being stoned a bit. In fact, my friends and I smoked pot, ate mushrooms, and dropped acid throughout high school. There was some cocaine in there as well. I don't say it to boast, because as an adult I can see the irreparable damage it can do to people. But although I don't do drugs now, truth be told, I had a great time. We didn't look at it as "doing drugs." We were just getting high and enjoying life. Some of my highs were so incredible that to this day I smile thinking about them. In their ground-breaking book, *Stealing Fire*, Steven Kotler and Jamie Wheal make a case that a good acid trip or dose of psilocybin mushrooms is much more effective and provides longer-lasting relief for PTSD than Prozac and other money-making drugs doled out by the drug companies. And the stigma of "smoking pot" in the '70s gave way to legal social acceptance in 2016. Maybe it's time to look at getting high differently? I don't know. What I do know is I got to get high, and I smiled a lot.

Like at any high school, we had a lot of jerks around. Of course, everyone was doing the best they could given what they'd been brought up with, but there were some real shitheads (funny, "shitheads" doesn't even come up with a little squiggly red line indicating a misspelling). They looked down on others, thinking they were better, and they were often flat-out mean. The druggies (me) were looked down on by the jocks, and the bandies (me) were looked down on by—well, everybody (unless we were marching on the football field, in which case we were all right). For the most part I was left alone and I wasn't a dick to anyone.

But I had my moments, and for the few kids I was less than kind to, making fun of them for their thick glasses, or weight, or whatever, I am sorry. As adults, I'm sure the shitheads are sorry, too.

Practice

Get out your high school yearbook. Find someone you were mean or unkind to. Find them on Facebook and apologize. Something like, "Hi Jane. In high school I was unkind to you. Peer pressure, drugs, being abused as a child, whatever, no excuse, I could have been nice. I'm sorry, and I hope life has been good to you."

Get To—Smile—Make up.

Drum major,
Upper Arlington Band, 1979.

Catching the baton under
my leg at halftime.
I might have been stoned.

High school graduation, 1980:
I'm far left with Tim, David, and Dean.

Yeah, pretty cool.

KAX: We were so cool.

Our debut single.

In concert at some
high school auditorium, 1979.

5. Get To Regret (Part 1)

"The more you are emptied of your physical abilities, the more you are filled with the strength of soul."
—*Thomas Moore*

In early summer 1980, Jamie and I were making out upstairs in my bedroom. Jamie had long brown hair, was short, sweet, cute, 16, and my first real love. Ahhh, first love. I wonder what would have happened had Jamie and I stayed together. Thirty-eight years later, and I'm still thinking about that. That I cheated on her with several other high school girls pretty much ended whatever fantasy I would have later in life about being with her. We did connect on Facebook recently, and she was sweet. I think she forgives me. But if I get stabbed at a book signing in Columbus, check her alibi. *Get To—Smile—First love!*

Anyway, it was 8 p.m. on a hot midsummer Ohio night. Mom was out to dinner with a boyfriend. Suddenly we heard, from the back yard, a scream and "Breathe motherfucker, breathe!" Jamie and I looked at each other and I said, "It's just Rick and some friends swimming in the pool. They're wasted." We laughed. Then there was more commotion, someone making a call on the phone hanging on the wall in the kitchen, giving our address, then slamming it back on the hook. *Ordering pizza?* I thought. I heard a siren off in the distance that began to get louder and louder. *What the....?*

My heart kicked into gear and I tore down the stairs. I ran out back and on the cement next to the pool lay Richard. My brother, Rick, was over him doing CPR. Just as I got to them, the paramedics arrived with a stretcher to take over.

I didn't know Richard well. He lived nearby and was one of Rick's friends. I was 17, he was 19. At that age, that's a lifetime apart. He was big-muscled, and I remember one time he came over and his shirt was unbuttoned halfway, and I saw he had chest hair. I thought, *Yuck, I hope that never happens to me.* But a nice enough guy as far as I could tell, and, as Rick's other friends could be rough, I remember Richard having a sweet nature (i.e., not smacking me on the head when he walked by). A group of them had been out partying and had come over to our house for a swim. Richard dived into the shallow end—and broke his neck. Instantly, this 19-year-old who had just graduated from high school, a track star with his life ahead, was quadriplegic. Paralyzed from the neck down.

One day several months later I left the house, and just down the street on the other side of the road, there was Richard in his front yard, in his wheelchair. Just sitting there, of course. The chair was a contraption of metal supports and bars and levers. Kind of like an old, rudimentary version of the chair I suppose Stephen Hawking used back in the '70s. I can't imagine it was motorized or that he was able to use his mouth to move it. As I got near, I looked at him, briefly, then looked away and drove on—and didn't wave. He couldn't wave. My Pinto couldn't mask my shame and as I drove I felt sick. I was probably on my way to Jamie's house to fool around. Or maybe to meet a friend to play tennis. Or use my fake ID and go buy beer. Richard wasn't going to do any of those things.

For the next year, before I moved out of the house to be a teenager in my own apartment, of the many, many times I drove by and saw Richard sitting out in his yard or driveway, never once did I wave, let alone stop to say hi or offer to play a game of chess. Or say, "Dude, I am so sorry this happened. What can I do for you?" I did nothing and, for that, I experience regret.

• • • •

On a side note, I've been challenged over the years about my brother, Rick, who dropped out and didn't see Mom and Dad for years on end. But in his defense, when the paramedics showed up, one of them apparently said something like, "Why'd you pull him out of the pool?" Rick said, "Because he was drowning and I had to save his life." "Yeah," said the paramedic, "but you also probably paralyzed him." Drunk and stoned, having just saved your friend's life, sitting on the side of a pool on a muggy Ohio summer night, an 18-year-old hearing this could have a change in attitude about life. I don't know. He gets to do it as he's doing it, for whatever reason. I get to have compassion for my bro either way.

Practice

For years, whenever I thought of Richard in his wheelchair and remembered driving by without stopping, my heart would almost skip a beat. But I have come to peace with that, and with other regrets I have in life. I know in my heart that in every instance I was doing the best I could at that time. I've learned it's okay to be okay with things I've done that I regret. Think of something you regret doing. Feel the uneasy feeling, the remorse you may have. As a human, you always have the choice to forgive others, and yourself.

Get To—Smile—Forgive.

Get To
6. Hitchhike Across the Country

*"I'm super happy to be experiencing
this chaos of life. It's beautiful."*
—*Josiah Hargadon*

Not long after graduation, as a present to myself, I decided with my friend Todd to hitchhike out west. California was the general destination, but we had some "friends of friends" in Colorado so we headed there as a start. With a couple hundred bucks and fake IDs, Todd and I were ready. We rode in Jamie's 1979 yellow Ford Fiesta, and she dropped us off on the shoulder of I-70 West, just outside the 270 outerbelt on the west side of Columbus. The saying "Go West, young man, go West" never had more meaning. I'll never forget sitting there on the side of the freeway that hot afternoon as she drove off, the cars zooming by and leaving a haze of exhaust in their wake. *Yeah, I get to do this*, I thought, *but it's crazy*. It was slow at first, but we caught a number of rides that got us down the road into Indiana. We slept in fields and grassy areas in local parks. Most of the people who picked us up were great. But others . . .

Somewhere in Illinois a guy in an old Ford pickup truck pulled over, and we threw our backpacks in the bed and jumped in. I was in the middle and Todd at the door. We were chatting along and doing fine when the guy put his hand on my leg. The three of us were cramped there in a row in the cab, so I didn't think much of it. We were still new and giddy, the AM radio playing a country tune. Then I looked over and saw he had only a towel draped across his lap, and that under it he had an erection.

"What the fuck?" I threw his hand off of my leg and told him to pull over. Todd, who didn't see the towel, said, "What do you mean—he can take us closer to St. Louis." We were in the middle of nowhere. I said sternly, "No, we're getting out here!" Todd and I argued with the guy continuing to rub my leg and Todd wanting to keep going. I prevailed and he pulled over. I stayed in the truck while Todd got our bags out of the back. (Hitchhiking rule #7: Be careful as you get out of a pickup truck with your bag in the back, as they might drive away with it.)

When I explained to Todd what had happened he said, "Geez man, sorry," and we came up with a hand-signal system we would use from then on whenever we got into a car: Rubbing your nose with your finger means okay. Rub your earlobe: Something's fishy. Cough loudly: Pull over as fast as possible. We sat at the side of the road, eventually laughing, with relief, at the whole thing.

Looking back, I wish I had been calm, told the guy not to touch me, respected that he got arousal from something different than I did, and allowed him to drive us to St. Louis. It didn't have to be that big of a deal—Todd and I were a couple of young, strong guys. The only danger was to our sensibilities. The beauty of it all is that I get to smile about it now!

We got to experience so many things those several months on the road. Mostly great human beings wanting to help a couple of kids out. Most of them simply said, "Pay it forward," although in different words, since I don't think that phrase had been invented yet. We also did a lot of walking. Once, just outside of Kansas City, we came upon a car full of—I am not kidding—nuns with a flat tire. They had been there for a while with a sign in the window saying "Help!" but to no avail. With no cell phones, that's what you did—you waited until help arrived. We arrived, and fixed it. They gave us food, hugs, and a boatload of karma.

On another occasion we were picked up by the highway patrol in Topeka, Kansas. The patrolman took us to a bus station and said, "You boys buy a ticket and get out of my state on a bus. If I see you on my highway again, you're going to jail." We bought a bus ticket to the Colorado state line.

Somewhere in eastern Colorado a group of hippies picked us up and wanted to take us to a farm to "hang out." I might have had a Get To mindset, but I said no because they were freaky. Todd said yes. They dropped us off at a gas station and said they would come back for us. I assume they went to buy drugs. As we sat there at the gas station I told Todd that when they came back I wouldn't get in the car. They were too crazy and strung out. Todd said he would go with them. We experienced an intense couple of hours together contemplating splitting up on the plains of Colorado—but they never came back. In retrospect I wish they had returned, because I think I would have gone. Life is too short not to get to experience whatever that would have been!

We made it to Denver and stayed with some friends for a few days, then headed further west to Aspen. There we stayed at a friend's brother's house several miles outside of town. He was a real-estate developer and his name was Jimmy Joe. He lived with his girlfriend. One morning we walked out his back door into the woods—and got lost. Aspen is in the middle of nowhere, and his house even more so. I guess we were thinking that if we hiked up to the top of the ridge behind his house, we would see the town. We didn't see it and, bad decision, decided to keep going, thinking we'd run into it. The mind of a 17-year-old is sometimes inexplicable. As night started to fall ten hours later, scared, hungry, and thirsty, we panicked and got cut up and bruised as we desperately made our way down a jungle-like ravine we thought might lead to people. It did, and eventually into the town. We found the Jeep that Jimmy Joe kept parked in town, and we knew he kept the keys in the ashtray. We were exhausted and desperate. We took it and drove back to the house. An hour later the home phone rang and the call went to the answering machine. It was Jimmy Joe: "Ted, Todd, are you there? Where's the Jeep? Did you take it? What's up?"

We should have picked up and explained. We didn't. Soon after that, Jimmy Joe and his girlfriend came in, livid. We tried to explain, showing the scrapes and cuts, but they weren't hearing it. "What the fuck were you thinking?" They were pissed. Silent the rest of the night and during the Jeep ride at six the next morning when they dropped us off in Glenwood Springs, a small town 40 miles from Aspen at the I-70 junction. They didn't say it as they drove off in a trail of dust, but I could hear them thinking, *And don't come back!*

We'd been sitting for a couple of hours at a local cafe contemplating our next move when a guy headed to Wyoming offered us a ride. Why not?

The four-hour ride was in the back of his pickup truck and ended at the Cheyenne Frontier Days celebration. When we arrived there was an onslaught of the sounds and smells of the rodeo. It was intense. The rodeo itself, with real cowboys, clowns, and bulls, was amazing. Columbus is nicknamed "the Cowtown," but I promise it had never held anything like this. It was an amazing three-day affair. We met and partied with some cowboys and cowgirls. The people were giving of food and couches to sleep on. It was a treasure of experiences.

As fun and adventurous as it all was, after three months on the road we were tired, and we slowly made our way back to Columbus to dive back into life as 18-year-olds.

● ● ● ●

During our travels, we slept on park benches and in the backs of parked pickups, on the floors of friends' houses—really, anywhere we wouldn't get wet or eaten. We met amazing people, and plenty of weirdos. At times we were scared shitless. At times we laughed out loud. We spent hours sitting on the sides of freeways and country roads with our thumbs out, often playing gin rummy—the draw and discard piles in different shoes. When a car pulled over we'd grab our things and run up to it, wondering what life would bring this time. It was such an adventure. I see a lot of kids sleeping on park benches in Hollywood and other places these days. I wonder if they are having a get to experience like I did. I knew I could always go back to a warm home and food in Columbus, so it's not the same as for the real destitute. But I do see a lot of backpackers "slumming it," and I know many of them are having the experience of a lifetime.

Practice

Think of an adventure you dream of doing: parachuting, climbing Mt. Kilimanjaro, backpacking through Europe, riding a bike across America, whatever it might be. Gather photos of what that looks like to you (from magazines or the Internet), then paste them on a poster board. That's what I used to do. (Some people call these "vision boards.") Or forget the cutting and go straight to Pinterest, although there is something about the hands-on version. However you do it, look at it every day.

Get To—Smile—Dream!

In my experience, dreams do come true.

7. Get To Regret (Part 2)

Each of us, as an adult, makes the choice to live or not. Not just how we live, but if we live. No amount of guilt or shame, no laws or religious dogmas change that basic choice.

This is a tough one.

When I was 15, I dated a girl two years older than I was. She had a sweet butterfly tattoo on the inside of her thigh. Yum. Her name was Julie and she was the sweetest, most carefree woman I knew. Julie taught me about sex. Other than the usual teenage male adventures looking at my brother's girly magazines I had found hidden in his room, I was pretty new to this stuff. Julie and I had a great time! It wasn't love, but we dated and spent a year together. We stayed friends, contacting each other every once in a while over the years.

Five years after high school—so, 1985—I received a letter from her that said, basically, "Ted, I want you to know that of all the regrets I have in life, the biggest one is that I didn't keep your baby." Whoa!!! What do you do with that? I had no idea she had gotten pregnant. Shit! And she had an abortion. Double shit! What is this thing called life? We Get To do it and then you get a letter like that.

In reply, I said I was sorry (duh), and we continued to correspond. Many years later, in 1999, Julie was living in San Diego and I went to visit. She was in a custody battle for her 11-year-old daughter (not mine), and I could tell it was painful. We had a sweet time together and said we'd stay in touch. Several weeks later she called to see if I could get together with her again. She was feeling crappy and needed a friend to hang out with. I didn't have time.

A month after that, I received an email from her mom saying Julie had committed suicide.

I was stunned and sat, quietly, looking at the computer screen. The sadness that I felt was so great that I couldn't cry. To say Julie was sweet and carefree is an understatement. Yes, we had sex, but more than that we just hung out together. Dad had turned the downstairs into a game room with orange-yellowish shag carpet, pool and foosball tables, pinball machine, lava lamps, and black-light posters of The Who and Jimi Hendrix and some with crazy swirly psychedelic designs—and Julie and I spent hours down there together. She introduced me to the first book I really read, that I "fell into": J. R. R. Tolkien's *The Hobbit*. Julie, in her bellbottoms and flowery shirt, and I would snuggle up on one of the many beanbag chairs and read (she was into The Lord of the Rings), and talk, and read, and talk. She made me laugh. Maybe we weren't in love, but I loved her. She headed off to college in Florida and that was that.

Even today, I feel that I might have been able to change things, had I taken the time to see her that day in 1999. Regret can run deep. I think of Julie often.

Practice

We all know people who have passed away. So many in my own life whom I knew personally: Larry, Ted, Tracy, Sarah, Dave, Ron, Kenny, and many more I haven't seen for a while, some of whom I don't even know are gone.

Each passing, and the associated grieving, is a reminder of how fleeting life can be. Remember some of the people you know, or even a specific person who has passed away. How did you meet them? What were some clumsy or difficult moments in your relationship? What were some of the best moments? If you could see them now, what would you reminisce about? What would you say that seemed lost to time when you realized they'd vanished from this life? How would they answer you—or at least, how would you hope they'd answer?

Feel sorrow, feel sad, but also feel the joy for the time you did have with them. Theodore Geisel (Dr. Seuss) said, "Don't cry because it's over. Smile because it happened." Feel compassion and gratitude for your own life.

Get To—Smile—Rest in peace, friend.

8. Get To Go to Prison

No matter how constrained you may feel, you're not. We're all free on the inside.

Prior to and after graduating high school in 1980, besides cleaning buildings I had a number of jobs: gas-station attendant, candle-sales rep (where, as you'll see later, my consciousness cracked open), grocery boy, landscape designer—er, I mean grass cutter. I worked at a car dealership cleaning cars, jockeying cars, pinstriping cars. I sold Amway. I also got a degree from the International Bartender Institute and began my career as a bartender, pouring drinks at a pizza joint in town. It was loud and smoke-filled and smelled like pepperoni and beer, and was busy. I was in heaven not only while serving drinks but even when it was slow and I was just chatting with people about life. The skills of bartending I was learning would have a profound effect on me throughout my life.

During those years I was dating a sweet girl named Debbie who received a job offer to run a copy shop in Reno, Nevada. She asked if I wanted to go. I said, "Hell yeah!" (This is a recurring theme in my life. Girl: "Ted, you want to go with me to such-and-such place to live?" Ted: "Hell yeah!") So I quit the pizza joint, said goodbye to Mom and Dad (and my life as I knew it), and, with all my belongings packed in a Mayflower moving van, jumped in Debbie's hot, white, brand-new, two-door, 1983 Pontiac Fiero and took a month-long trip to Reno via Colorado, Arizona, San Diego (a place I vowed to return to someday), and up the coast of California. I'm sure many of you have driven across the country or taken long road trips, so you remember the long drives, the AM radio stations, the miles and miles of farmland, the majestic mountains. There's a great book called *Breakfast with Buddha* with a delicious narrative on driving out west. So with that book and your memories, you're in good hands in reliving a fantastic road trip. I'll spare you mine.

But I will share with you one wild thing we got to do: visit a guy I knew who was staying at Fort Leavenworth, Kansas. This is a United States Army installation located north of the city of Leavenworth. Built in 1827, it is the oldest continuously active military reservation west of the Mississippi River. It also houses the Department of Defense's only maximum-security prison. This is where Craig was. Here's the story as I remember it.

Craig, a kid in my class in high school, had been convicted of attempted murder while he was in the army. Apparently, they have these things called blanket parties where all the guys in the barracks throw a blanket over someone and beat and kick the crap out of him. The target is usually the barracks bully, but according to some things I've read, they often target suspected gays. Regardless, it's shitty, and the kid almost died. Or maybe he did die? I don't know.

Anyway, Craig, a 19-year-old kid himself, was the only one convicted (scapegoat?), and he got time in maximum security at Fort Leavenworth. Although I didn't know him well, when word got around in Columbus about it, I sent him a letter—and became his pen pal. We corresponded often, sharing stories about our lives. A year later I told him I had met Debbie and that we would be driving past Leavenworth on our way to Reno, and I asked if he'd mind if we stopped by. He was thrilled.

Debbie and I arrived on a beautiful spring day, windows down, singing along to Devo's "Whip It" as we drove up to the prison. ("Whip it, whip it good!" we sang out loud.) As we got closer to the ominous building complex and noticed the 20-foot-tall, five-foot-thick rock walls with guard turrets and razor-wire on top, we quieted down. When we pulled up to the guard gate and the man there asked me for my ID, we became silent. This guy was not fucking around. After asking a bunch of questions that seemed to be testing my honesty, he checked some paperwork, then nodded to a stone-faced soldier who opened the gate. We drove into the compound. As we parked in front of the huge prison walls with giant metal doors blocking anyone from getting out, or in, it hit me: Craig was living in there.

Today, on the Fort Leavenworth website, it states: "We look forward to serving you upon your arrival and hope that your experience, while living or visiting here, leaves a lasting impression as you enjoy the 'Best Hometown in the Army.'" I'm sure Fort Leavenworth left a lasting impression on Craig!

In those days, I didn't have a website to prep me for what was to come, and I was too busy getting high and getting laid during our road trip to think about Craig's reality. I wish I had kept the letters from Craig, because I know he told me about the hell he was living in. But like most of us do when reading about another's shitty situation, until we see it in person, it doesn't sink in. Craig's reality was sinking in.

I don't recall the exact procedure for getting in, but I do remember a series of thick metal doors, ID checks, and pat-downs.

The guards were big, bearish, and . . . scary. I remember thinking that any of them could snap me like a twig. I had jumped out of airplanes, hitchhiked across the country, and played pool in the slums, but still, let's be honest—I was a naive pussy. That's what we called it back then when you peed your pants when facing scary situations. I don't recall necessarily peeing my pants, but I was still a big fat pussy.

Debbie and I were sitting in the dark, dank waiting area when a large metal door squeaked open and Craig emerged, guard in tow. We hugged. He smiled and held himself strong, saying he was doing okay. But I could see the strain on his face, betraying the challenges he'd endured.

He was a good kid in a really bad situation. I can only imagine what had happened to him in there. In truth, maybe it was nothing. We never talked about it. We chatted for a bit about general stuff. It's not like we had been best friends in high school, so it was a little awkward. I was with a girl on my way to the West Coast to party, and he was going back into a jail cell. But it was a powerful experience for me, and I know in my heart it meant a lot to him.

As we walked out of that intense, confined place and into the Kansas sun, I felt so free. To Craig, and all the veterans—my sister Julie, her husband, and my nephew Colin included—thank you for that! Fighting for our freedom, which I got to experience so profoundly in that moment—thank you. (There's usually a vet standing at the freeway exit ramp on my way home from work—I think I'll give him some money tonight.)

I kept in touch with Craig for a few years, until he got released. In one letter a few years later he said he had a girlfriend and was drinking a beer while writing to me and I thought, "Okay, he's getting laid and otherwise enjoying the realities of being human. He'll be fine." I haven't heard from him in 30 years. All the best to you, Craig.

Practice

The experience with Craig had a huge effect on me. More than 2 million people are sitting in U.S. jails today, many for things they did and regret. The awful food, the empty feeling of missing loved ones day after day, wishing they could redo the past. Sit quietly for ten minutes and feel your own freedom.

Get To—Smile—Experience being free.

9. Get To Bartend

People who drink, and people who don't drink, are all just trying to be happy.

As I've said, bartending has helped define my way of being, of how I view life. At bartender's school, it was more than just learning what went into drinks. A drink was soul food, and how it was crafted, with care and understanding, was the ultimate acknowledgement of another person's needs. Bartending is about learning to relate to people, to be attentive and listen. We don't get much attention, but we do play a big role in many people's lives.

A well-made drink is a work of art. Think about this: The bartender in the James Bond films who makes the perfect martini barely gets noticed . . . but can you imagine if he did a bad job? Scene: Interior of a high-class casino in Monaco. The camera pans across the cigar-hazed room, where sharply dressed men and high-heeled, evening-gown-clad women, obvious high rollers, are playing poker and baccarat. We slowly zoom in on the bar, where James is speaking intimately with a woman in a long black evening gown, auburn hair flowing down her back. James has eyed, over her shoulder, a tuxedoed man, the outline of a gun suggested under his blazer, surveying Bond from a distance. We tune in to the conversation in time to hear the woman ask, with a slight grin and in a seductive voice, "Shall we, Mr. Bond? My place or yours?" James, in his debonair way, reaches for the martini glass, smiles wryly, winks at the bartender, looks at the woman, takes a sip, and after a beat says, "Bloody hell, too much vermouth."

When we arrived in Reno, I quickly learned that, contrary to my short-lived belief, it's very difficult to make a living gambling. After a few quick, lucky wins at the blackjack tables, I got cocky and lost all of my $1,000 savings. Gambling is tricky that way: you win just enough to keep you going until you've lost it all.

After several weeks of living off Debbie, I found a job at the MGM Grand Casino/Hotel, which at the time was one of the largest casinos in the world. I wanted to jump in right away as a bartender, but that's not how it works. I started out on one of the lower rungs of the ladder as a bar porter, which is basically a guy who cleans the bar itself.

I would arrive for my shift at 2 a.m., put on a gray smock, take a large metal cart from the basement up a huge, smelly service elevator to the bars on the casino floor, pick up the foul-smelling, heavy rubber floor mats, take them down to the basement and hose them off, come back up and lay them back down. I would then do the same with the incredibly gross trash cans. Thirty-three years later I can still smell that rank odor. But I had been a janitor, and I could handle all the scrubbing and smells. What was challenging, though, was when I arrived at the bar and the bartenders and waitresses would snicker at the new guy (me) as they got out of my way so I could clean. When, in my jovial way, I said hi to the waitresses, they rolled their eyes and looked the other way. I was trash to them. It was demoralizing beyond words. Several weeks in, I called Mom from the cafeteria pay phone, crying my eyes out, saying, "I can't do it anymore!" But Mom, bless her heart (although it gave out on her and she died because of it), told me to hang in there. I did.

It took a year, but I made my way through the ranks, from a gray-smocked porter to a red-vested "bar back," stocking the bar and shagging ice for the bartender. The waitresses talked to me and actually gave me the time of day. Soon after that I graduated from the required five-month-long MGM bartender's school (my degree in mixology from the International Bartender Institute in Columbus didn't cut it) and finally got into the coveted, gold-studded black vest on one of the main casino bars. Although it was the 2 a.m. graveyard shift, it was an amazing journey of learning to let go of expectations and appreciate each moment in life. The feeling was much like the one I had cleaning buildings—that there are so many people living their lives in their own way, and I really am no different. We get to experience life just as it's unfolding for us.

Bartending on the main casino bar at the MGM Grand Hotel was one of the most eye-opening periods of my life. The rich, the poor, the drunks, the hookers, and everyone in between would find their way to my bar. I would serve each one with care. Night after night, I experienced incredible humans, being just—incredible. One time, a guy sat at the bar drinking, throwing black and green chips at me. If I caught them, I got to keep them. If I dropped them, I bought him a drink. We played for hours. The green chips were $25 and the black chips were $100. I don't think he knew or cared. I made thousands of dollars. He got wasted, and I kept smiling and thinking, *I get to do this for a living?*

On another occasion, I came on for my 2 a.m. shift and was called into the manager's office. "Yes sir?" I asked.

"Ted, was there a guy at your bar last night with a red sweater, glasses, and a cowboy hat?" he asked seriously.

"Yeah, sure. A guy named Bernard, or Bart. Anyway, he mortgaged his house and came to gamble. Lost it all. He was at my bar drowning his sorrows. He sure could drink," I laughed.

My manager didn't laugh. He said, "Bernard, or Bart, was found unconscious on the floor next to a slot machine this morning. He's in the hospital." Shit. There's a certain responsibility when serving drinks that I learned that night. I trust that Bernard, or Bart, ended up okay and that life has taken a better turn for him.

Practice

Grab a glass of your favorite beverage—a glass of wine or a beer, or a stiff martini. Or a glass of orange juice. Deliberately put the glass to your lips and slowly let the liquid enter your mouth. Exhale through your nose and notice how the flavor changes as the aromatic particles pass through your nostrils. Swallow, and be aware of how the taste and temperature change as it passes over your tongue and drains down your throat. As the moments pass, notice the sensation as the alcohol or the sugar enters your bloodstream. Embrace the experience.

Get To—Smile—Liquid buzz!

MGM Grand, 1985. The black vest!

Debbie and Pat, Reno, 1985.

10. Get To Wake Up

*I am going to San Diego with a drive
and will that is unstoppable.*
—*Journal entry, Reno, September 5, 1985*

There was a lot of partying in Reno. When we got off work at 10 a.m., a group of us would go to the mountains in Lake Tahoe and ski (in the winter) or whitewater raft (in the summer), drinking, smoking pot, and snorting coke the whole way. If the weather was bad, we'd simply go to some casino and gamble and party the day away. Being locals, we knew where the cheap drinks and easy slots were. Someone always had a friend somewhere who would get us a handful of free drink tickets. There was wild abandon in most of what we did. We slogged our way home, went to sleep at 7 p.m., woke up at 1 a.m. and started all over again.

But then my best friend from high school, Pat, moved out from Columbus to stay with me. He'd also gotten a job at the MGM—and he saved my life. I had been in Reno for about a year when he arrived on the scene. After a few weeks, we were at a local casino bar drinking, and he said, "I have to tell you Ted, if I met you now, I wouldn't be your friend."

"What the fuck do you mean?" I asked defensively.

He said, "You're dead. You're smoking pot, snorting coke, drinking like a fish. You're hanging out and having fun and all, but where's the 'live life on the edge' Ted I used to know? If you keep this up, you're literally going to be dead."

I was dumbfounded. I held Pat's gaze. In that moment, in the midst of the clattering of slot machines, the whoops and hollers from a nearby craps table, everything got quiet—and I changed. I think we all have moments in life where we wake up, where we get a "whack on the side of the head" (which is the title of a great book by the way), and there's a shift in consciousness, a deciding moment where you'll do something or become someone you weren't before. It's a moment when you decide to quit smoking or drinking, or decide to learn a language, or climb a mountain. It can be subtle, but it's powerful. *Whack!*

Within days I had decided to get a real-estate license. Nevada is known for having one of the hardest real-estate tests to pass, but I was undeterred. I took a course in real estate at the Reno community college, studied for six months, and finally took the state test. The results took several weeks to arrive. On a snowy winter night on the way in to work at 1 a.m., Pat and I stopped at the bank of mailboxes in the apartment-complex office, and there was the letter from the Nevada Real Estate Board. We sat in my car shivering, and with cold, shaking hands, I slowly opened the envelope. We were quiet as I unfolded the paper inside, as though we knew something life-changing was there, but we couldn't put our finger on it. A score of 70 was the passing grade. I had a 68. I had failed it by a single two-point question.

My frown of disappointment at failing slowly turned into a smile of understanding. During the test I had made a change to just one answer, and I realized at that moment my first answer had been correct. I showed Pat and we sat quietly for a few moments. Finally I said, "Remember I told you how much I loved San Diego? Well, I'm done here and ready to move."

He said, "Yeah, me too. I'm going back to Columbus. I can go with you to San Diego before I head east."

I said, "I'm giving my two-week notice tonight." Pat said, "Ditto." And just like that, my two-year adventure was over. I packed up all my stuff, said goodbye to Debbie (we had long since broken up), and, with Pat leading the way in my new Ford Taurus, I headed south in a U-Haul truck.

Practice

I've been reading lately about the benefits of not eating grain. The problem is, I'm a bread-aholic. Regardless, lately I decided to not have any bread or chips or anything made with grain for one month. I'm two weeks in. The other day my 12-year-old boy made pancakes by himself for the first time. I asked for a bite. He said, "Dad, that's cheating on your no-bread diet." I told him that my decision to not eat bread for 30 days is strong, and that one bite of my son's first pancakes won't send me down the road to hell.

This is not to discount the incredible challenges addicts of all kinds have, where one drink or puff can actually be a road to hell. But for things like bread and exercise—or choosing to be attentive to your kids—deciding to do it sometimes only takes a whack and doesn't need to be that serious.

Are you ready for a whack? Right—now think of something you want to do in your life. Got it?

No "Yeah but."

No "Ok, but later."

No anything. Commit to doing it for 30 days. *Just commit*. Don't try. Just do it. Yoda said it perfectly: "Do or do not, there is no try." If you want to take a bite of your kid's first pancakes two weeks in, you know what? You'll be fine—just keep going. After 30 days, decide if you want to do it for another 30 days. Right now, if you're smiling, maybe even a little smugly, you'll know you decided, and it will be a reality for you.

Okay, ready? *Get To—Smile—Do it!*

Congratulations!

11. Get To San Diego

San Diego is fantastic.
Life is fantastic.
I made $20 in tips working at the
Sheraton today. Hey bartender!
—*Journal entry, San Diego,*
November 13, 1985

The U-Haul truck ran out of gas somewhere on State Route 395 midway down the east side of the Sierra Nevada Mountains that run up the spine of California. Later we learned it had a busted gas gauge. But otherwise it was an uneventful journey, with the immense mountains, Yosemite snuggled within, passing by on my right, and thoughts of a new life keeping a nervous smile on my face.

Pat stayed for a few days before I dropped him at the San Diego airport and, for the first time, I got to be alone in the world. My U-Haul in the parking lot of a cheap hotel ten miles east of the ocean I had come for, I scoured newspapers for apartments and jobs. I met a lot of people offering one or the other, but without an apartment address I couldn't get a job, and without a job, I couldn't get an apartment. I sobbed myself to sleep for many nights, scared shitless as I was slowly running out of cash. But after a week, I found a crappy apartment with a couple of guys I begged to allow me to move in with and again found gainful employment bartending. First, I poured beer for the San Diego Chargers football games. When I went from the black-diamond-studded vest to another gray smock, this time worn behind a beer cart at a football stadium, my ego took a hit. It was stinky and the smell of stale beer I'd loved in the High Street bars in Columbus made me want to puke. The people were rude, and I wondered where I was heading in life. Each touchdown that brought a roar from the crowd, as I slopped dirty rags on the counters of a cart in the cement hallways of the stadium, depressed me. When a drunk, belligerent fan wearing a San Diego jersey and a backward baseball cap would laugh with his friends and say, "Yo, can't you fuckin' get a head on that beer?" I felt defeated. Is this what I had traveled across the country for? Moving back to Columbus was not far from my mind.

But after three months, eking out just enough money to pay rent at my cockroach-infested apartment and applying at dozens of places, I finally found a job bartending at the Sheraton Grand Hotel at the Harbor Island Marina. I was back to a black vest— and waitresses. I was in heaven yet again. We partied a lot. I laughed a lot. I made great friends whom I haven't seen now in 20 years: Mia, Mara, Trish, Sheila, and Doug, where are you? We went sailing during the days with the regulars who hung out at the bar and had boats moored at the marina below. The days were ours: bike rides to Tijuana, Mexico, for lunch, jai alai and the greyhound dog-race track; surfing and tennis. I'd thought Reno was "get-to" fun—this was get-to funner! Life unfolding each moment was a miracle of adventures. I moved from my apartment in the valley to a house a few blocks from the beach, sharing it with a couple of very cool guys. One of them, Mike, had lived in Singapore teaching English for a few years and told me stories about his adventures. I thought, *I would love to live in Asia!* But I had some things to do first.

Practice

Like the slow, imperceptible rising and falling of mountains, a human life is a slow, undetectable evolution created by the multitude of thoughts and beliefs someone has over time. Look at your younger life and see if you can find patterns that have led to who you are today. A voracious reader with a troubled childhood will see the path that led to becoming a writer. The lonely kid who imagined lives for his plastic army-men, and who later spent lunch breaks and study hall in the art room, might see the path that led to their becoming an art therapist. Where did you come from? Where are you going?

Get To—Smile—Be who you are.

12. Get To Pilot's License

Yes, I just had my first flying lesson.
I love the air. I love to fly.
Life feels really good.
— *Journal entry, San Diego,*
September 29, 1986

Determined not to get too lost in the party life (as I had in Reno), I studied for—and this time passed—the state's real-estate exam. I sold a house. I showed one couple ten different houses. They complained about everything: The layout is wrong, the color is wrong, the wallpaper is wrong. "Are you fucking *kidding* me?" I wanted to yell at them. "Paint it!" But I held my tongue. The house they did choose was a nightmare of a negotiation. So I quit.

Real estate was not my cup of tea, so I invented a portable screen door. To sell it, I decided, I would need a pilot's license to get around to all the stores. Looking back, that was really a silly excuse since I didn't actually have a product yet—but it was enough for my mind to justify getting a pilot's license. Flight time was expensive, so I got a second job fueling planes at the local airport, Montgomery Field, which allowed me a discount on flying lessons. I was busy bartending at night, developing the portable screen door in the mornings, working at the airport during the days, and studying avionics in between, but I was in heaven because I was in the Get To frame of mind.

My instructor, Tom, was a young guy just trying to get flight time so he could fly the big jets one day. We were buds and had a great time together. So, after just four months of study and flying, he decided I was ready for my final checkout flight—the one with an ex-military pilot who decides if you're fit to have a license. I think his name was Judd, but honestly I don't remember. I do remember his scary leather flight jacket covering a robust belly and his dark Ray-Bans.

On the day of the flight, we went out to the plane, did the preflight walk around, checking the wings, the tires, the propeller. Checked that there was gas. Duh. No problem. We climbed in and got our headphones on, and Judd said, "Are you ready?"

"Ready!" I said. I contacted the tower and taxied to the runway. Systems check, checklist check, check check check, ready for takeoff. We were in a Piper Archer airplane, which has one propeller and seats four people. Pretty straightforward to fly. "Ah, Montgomery Tower, Piper eight-Charlie-Papa at runway 28 left, ready for takeoff, over."

"Ah, roger that Piper, runway 28 left, cleared for takeoff… Um, good luck." I think that tower controller was smiling and knew I was fucked.

Judd and I rolled down the runway and at just the right time I pulled the yoke back and we lifted off. About 20 seconds in, as we got to about 1,000 feet, just over the 805 freeway, Judd reached over and pulled the throttle to "off." He'd cut the power to the engines! We started to drop. I screamed, "What the fuck?" and reached over and pushed the power back on. He yelled, "What are you doing?" and pulled the lever back down. I almost shit my pants with fear. "What, what, what?" I screamed. He pushed the power back on, saying sternly, "I've got it!" and took control of the plane.

A few thudding heartbeats later I realized he'd performed an emergency exercise I'd done many times with Tom, in which he would suddenly create a power failure by pulling the throttle off, thus simulating a failed engine. I would then take action, like tilting the nose down, trimming the flaps, checking the ignition, battery and other gauges in rapid sequence to determine what was wrong. If there was no fixing the engine, I'd pretend to glide the plane to a point where you might be able to land (in a field without wires or fences, on a freeway or road) and survive. This would all happen in five seconds, and then you'd push power back on and keep going. But I wasn't prepared when Judd did it, so I freaked out.

Judd was not happy, and, as a former sergeant in the Marines, he must have wanted to kick the shit out of me.

We finished the checkout flight and landed, taxiing to our parking spot—in silence. He got out and went to the terminal while I did the post-flight airplane rundown: chocks on the wheels, tie downs, look for nicks on the propeller, visually inspect the wings, etc. When I finally walked into the small office, where six or so people were milling around, it was silent and no one looked at me. I had worked there fueling planes for four months by now and knew everyone, and you could feel the negative energy. I looked over and there on the desk was my check-out report and in big letters: FAILED. In a back room we heard yelling. It was Judd reaming Tom a new one. I guess Judd didn't think he trained me like Judd thought he should have. I felt like shit, not only for failing, but for disappointing Tom.

A few days later, Tom and I met, talked about what went wrong and returned to the air, practicing emergency procedures—

during takeoff!—and a month or so later I had another check-out. Judd was, luckily, off that day so I had another, nicer guy who passed me. But truth be told, with only 49 hours of flight time in five months of flying, I should not have been given a pilot's license. I wasn't ready. As incredibly enjoyable as it was from that day on, flying with my friends up to Big Bear Mountain to ski for the day, or out to Catalina Island for lunch, or even to Las Vegas to spend time with a friend, I had no business up in the air.

For example: *Pilot's log, March 4, 1989—Forgot alt. setting leaving Big Bear.* One time, after a day of skiing in the southern California mountains, three of my favorite waitresses and I loaded our skis and other equipment back in the plane, piled in, and got ready for takeoff. Half way down the runway we hadn't left the ground yet and I was thinking, *Shit, I should abort.* At higher altitudes there is less air pressure, and thus less lift. We were too heavy. My heart was pounding, but I kept going. We finally left the ground, but we were only "flying" due to ground effect: a cushion of air between the wings and runway keeps you off the ground but you're not really flying—as soon as there's no ground underneath it, the airplane drops. We were only ten feet off the ground. The end of the runway came, and the lake, and for a few moments it seemed we were in ground effect over the lake. But we kept flying and started gaining altitude. I was sick to my stomach but kept it together. I was the pilot, after all. That evening, back at the bar, stunning customers because we had gone snow skiing, come home and gone surfing, and were now pouring drinks on the bar, I never mentioned the nearly fatal flying I had done.

Pilot's log, July 12, 1989—Lost comm. on return flight—we were late for Al Jarreau. I shouldn't tell another story, but I will. My girlfriend, Marlene (whom I'll introduce shortly), was living up in L.A., and for her birthday I bought tickets to an Al Jarreau concert in San Diego. I said I would fly up and get her and fly back down. Feeling ever so cool, on the day of the concert I flew up and met her as planned. Everything was fine. I was the cool pilot after all, but right after takeoff my radios went out—I lost comms. Zero communications with the tower. *Shit!*

On takeoff from the Orange County John Wayne Airport near Los Angeles, you head out over the coast, turn left, and follow the shoreline 80 miles to San Diego. It's a pretty easy task, really. So we did that, but the whole time, I was fiddling with the radios without luck. It was getting dark, and at some point Marlene, who was totally relaxed, said, "Isn't that downtown San Diego ahead?" OMG! I was about to fly into the main San Diego Airport air space. So I banked hard left to head inland. With fate or luck or angels, I was on the right flight path to Montgomery Field. And with fate or luck or angels, just as I was getting close to the airport, thinking I'd have to land without talking to the tower, the radio crackled on—"heading east at Mt. Soledad, contact tower immediately. Repeat, aircraft heading east at Mt. Soledad, *contact Montgomery tower immediately.*" What a relief!

I replied, "Ah, Montgomery tower, this is Piper seven-eight-Charlie-Papa, request permission to land."

"Piper, this is Montgomery tower, we've been calling you! Cleared for landing."

I got to believe in fate, luck AND angels that night. (Note: Montgomery Airport is right next to the Navy's Miramar "Top Gun" flight-training school. If this had been post 9/11, I'm pretty sure I would have been shot down.)

Oh, as for the portable screen door, I saw it at Home Depot nearly 15 years later—but it wasn't mine. Back then, I had prototypes made and showed it to a few potential investors, but it never went anywhere. I guess I still wanted to be a bartender.

Practice

Today, air travel is not quite the exotic thing it was in the past. We often take it for granted. Nevertheless, it is an amazing feat of human endeavor. I remember the '70s, when airplane crashes were almost common. In 1985, while I was living in Reno, an airliner crashed on takeoff, killing 71 people just a few miles from our apartment. Debbie and I heard the explosion at 1 a.m. and ran out of the house to see the flames in the distance. These days, crashes are rare, and when they do happen—well, witness what "Sully" did on the Hudson River in 2009: he ditched a crippled plane in the river, and all 155 people survived. The safety protocols and training of crews is astounding. I remain in awe of it all.

Next time you're in an airplane, sit at the window and look out. Marvel at the magnificence of what you're doing. There you are, in a tube hurtling through the sky at 500 mph.

Get To—Smile—Fly!

The cool pilot...

... and the waitresses from the bar.

Over Big Bear Lake where we
almost went in the water. Scary.

13. Get To Write a Book

The question is not what you're going to do with your life, it's how you are going to be in your life every moment.

One day, as I came into the bar lounge at the Sheraton for my night shift, I noticed a cute girl playing the piano and singing. Ah, the new lounge act. Her name was Marlene. She was hot! She had a boyfriend up in L.A., but forget that, she was on a three-month gig in San Diego, and there was no turning back. We fell in love. In between song sets she would sit at the bar and I'd serve her wine and we would talk—for hours. We played during the days. We were like peas in a pod. She was Cuban and opened my eyes to an entire way of being, of loving, of being passionate about life. She taught me Spanish: *Hola mi amor!* She asked what I was aspiring to do, post–real estate and pilot's license, and I said, "Be a bartender." She said, "No, there's more to life for you." I said, "I get to do this thing called life and either as a bartender, pilot, janitor, or businessman, it is all part of living it. A bartender is as good as any, so: I get to be a bartender!" She repeated, "There's nothing wrong with being a bartender, but there's more for *you*." To this day we're great friends and still argue about that point, although I think it turns out she was right.

After six months of completely random, crazy playing, Marlene decided to move back to L.A. and said, "Do you want to move up here with me?" In typical fashion I said, "Hell, yeah!" But instead of going up to L.A. to bartend, I had a great idea:

There are no good books on babysitting. I'm going to write one. So I gave notice at the Sheraton and moved up to L.A. to write and publish a book. Since we were living in West Hollywood I had to do the Hollywood thing, so I took an acting class and auditioned for a couple of television commercials. I sucked. I then got a job as a tour guide at Universal Studios. The first day on the job it was summer, sweltering hot, and standing on that tram, making announcements to those Midwest tourists, who reminded me that I, too, was a Midwest tourist, made me sick. I quit. Book publishing it was. On June 1, 1988, after nine months of development, I self-published *The Babysitters Business Guide*. It was a very simple book consisting of basic information on baby-sitting (I was, after all, an expert, as I had been babysat many, many times in life). I sold 800 copies. Breakeven was 10,000. I got to experience disappointment and went back to bartending, this time getting hired on to open a new, swanky Beverly Hills restaurant bar called Tribeca. I poured drinks for Cher on opening night, and once again was in my element and King of the Bar. There are photos of Billy Joel and Elton John having dinner there sometime later. But I didn't get to meet them because two weeks after starting, the job ended.

This is why. Marlene came home one night from her gig at a restaurant lounge in Santa Monica and said, "I got a job offer to play the piano in Osaka, Japan." A few cocktails later (those were the real drinking days), she asked, "Do you wanna come with me?" I said, in about as drunk a voice as there is, "Wheeeere's Japan?" She said, in an equally drunk voice, "On the other side of Hawaii. Wanna come?" "Hellll yeah!" There it was again! Bankrupt from the failed book, I thought, why not?

Two weeks later we packed everything up and put it in a storage room for $60 a month. Marlene headed over first, and after a week visiting my family in Columbus, I followed. The adventure was about to begin. I was about to get to do so many incredible things, get to experience a reality that was beyond anything this kid from Columbus knew could happen.

Practice

Start a journal. Get a notebook, set a timer, and write for 20 minutes. Do this every day for 30 days. Don't reread any of it until after the 30 days. Then read what you've written. Edit it a bit if you want, but don't get too caught up. Now go to Amazon's CreateSpace or IngramSpark and publish it for free. You don't have to make it publicly available—you can just order a copy for yourself if you like. Hold that copy in your hands, run your thumb over the cover, appreciate the fact that your thoughts and aspirations for those 30 days are worth something. Not necessarily to the public, but to you as a human being.

Get To—Smile—Write a book!

The Sheraton San Diego, 1987.

The Babysitters Business Guide

CARING FOR CHILDREN
professionally

By TED LARKINS

I sold 800 copies—
not quite enough.

14. Get To Japan

Life unfolds in front of us every moment, and we never know which of those moments will be life changing. So I work at smiling at all of them.

I arrived in Osaka on a cool October night in 1988. The immigration process was seamless and efficient, and everything was new and clean. In fact, everything was immaculate. (On a later trip to India, I would come to appreciate just how clean and efficient Osaka was.) Marlene met me at baggage claim and, after gathering my many suitcases, we got into a waiting taxi. It was shiny and new, but the driver, decked out in white gloves, didn't speak a word of English. I thought, *How am I going to get around this place?* Marlene handed him a piece of paper with an address on it, so that was a start. My heart was pounding with excitement as we drove down the smallest of roads and back alleyways, eventually arriving at the apartment that had been arranged for her.

Life unfolds in front of us every moment, and we never know which of those moments will be life changing. Osaka offered a few. Here's one of them.

I woke up the next morning, noticing Marlene had already gone out, and I smiled knowing I was up to my own devices to explore.

So I wrote a postcard to Mom with a short, cryptic message: "If you're reading this, I made it to the Osaka post office by myself and mailed this on my first day in Japan. Know that it was an adventure. Love, Ted."

I headed out the door, and ran into an old woman mopping the floor in the lobby. I smiled at her, she smiled back, slightly bowed, and said, *"Ohio."*

I was stunned. "Yes!" I said. "Yes, I'm from Ohio!"

She chuckled and said, "Oh, no, no, no. *Ohio* means 'good morning' in Japanese."

What? Are you *kidding* me? How easy is this language? Sushi, Kamikaze, Ohio—*I can learn this!* I thought. At that moment, the belief that Japanese was easy to speak took hold in my mind and paved the way for the coming 25 years of my life. I left her, smiling and saying "ohio" to everyone I met, even the post office guy who, with great patience, assisted me in getting my postcard stamped and mailed.

Life in Japan those first few months was wild. There was an indescribable smell in the air that I've come to learn is so "Japan." I soaked it in at every turn. The whole scene was a fantastical bombardment of sights and smells, sounds and... tastes. Of course there was sushi and ramen, but there was also *okonomiyaki* (cabbage-and-egg mixture grilled with squid on top), *kushikatsu* (a variety of meats and vegetables skewered on small sticks and deep fried), and *oyaku donbori* (a chicken-and-fried-egg mixture over rice). This was 1988, and it was far from the normal Columbus, Ohio, fare I'd grown up on. I was in heaven, but Mars was yet to come.

I bartended, taught English, and had various other jobs. At that time, foreigners were rare in Osaka, so I was picked to model for a clothing brand, emcee a fashion show, be a contestant on a late-night game show, and be an extra for a national railway TV commercial. I even worked at a grocery store handing out samples of tofu, kids and adults alike staring at the strange, smiling foreigner in the kimono. The entire time I was immersed in the language.

One night during those first months, I was out to dinner with a fellow American who had lived in Osaka for a number of years. He was complaining that someone had teased him about his Osaka accent, better known as Osaka-ben. I said, "Are you kidding me? You get to speak Japanese, and you're worried about getting teased about your Osaka-ben? I would die to speak Japanese well enough to even have an accent." In my mind, I screamed at him, *You get to do this!* but he couldn't hear me.

Three months into our life there, visiting shrines, Zen temples, and fish markets and simply grocery shopping with the masses, Marlene said, "Ok, I'm ready to move back to L.A. My gig is up, and I'm going back to L.A. to be a star. Wanna come?"

I looked at her, and for the first time in my life I didn't say "Hell, yeah!" I simply said, "Sayonara. I'm going to stay here in Japan."

Practice

Make a list of the countries you'd like to visit. Pick your favorite one, and write a date six months from now as the day you'll land there. Start planning. Even if you know you can't go, look up flight times and write them down. Make actual reservations for things that don't require a deposit and can be canceled without penalty: car reservations, hotel reservations, city tours. Get a beginner's guide to the language and learn a new word every day. Learn about the food they serve there, and if you can, visit a restaurant in your area that serves that type of food. Ask for specific dishes you've learned about, and if the server is from there, strike up a conversation. Watch a classic film made in the native language of the place you want to visit (make sure it's subtitled, not dubbed!).

Get To—Smile—Explore!

Marlene and me. First days in Osaka, 1988.

At a park near Yoshida's house
in Osaka, 1990. I loved the kids.

Teaching English, Community
Plaza English School, Osaka, 1989.

15. Get To Homestay

Every time you say "I believe" or "I think" such and such, you stop being able to experience someone else's reality.

Here's the deal: I didn't have a college degree, and the ability to speak fluent Japanese seemed like a great tool to have in my life arsenal. Staying in Japan was the only way to do that, and besides, it felt like our relationship had run its course. It was time for Marlene to move on (she felt that way, too).

I also had a goal. Marlene had been teaching me Spanish for two years, and I was now three months into learning Japanese. I decided I would study both languages full time, then go to Spain and translate for the 1992 Barcelona Olympics. Even today, I'm grateful for my naiveté in things like this. Had I known the task would be so daunting—read, "impossible"—I never would have tried. But I didn't know, and . . . it was a great dream to have.

With Marlene's impending departure, I decided to look for a homestay where I could learn Japanese better. I told my customers at the bar, the Wild West Club (where I was the token Spanish-speaking *gaijin*—Japanese for "foreigner"), what I was considering. There was an English-speaking customer at the bar named Muraki, and he said he knew a guy looking to have a *gaijin* stay at his home for free in exchange for teaching his kids English. It would be for three months. So one dark, rainy night, we all met at the lobby lounge in the Osaka, Miyako Hotel. The guy's name was Yoshida. He didn't speak English, but by then I had added a number of words to my "Ohio" vocabulary, so we figured it out. Muraki made the introductions and translated for a few minutes.

The next thing I knew, I was in Yoshida's car, and we were heading to his house. We went inside and he introduced me to his wife, Mitsuko, and their two boys. She looked at me—coldly. They started talking. Now, I'm no genius, but even I can tell the difference between arguing and a friendly conversation. It was not quite yelling, but definitely arguing.

This went on for 30 minutes, and then Yoshida looked at me, smiled, and said, *"Irashai,"* which I knew meant "welcome." Mitsuko walked away without saying anything. My eyes were as big as saucers at what was happening, and I just sat there—stunned—and nervously smiled. Two weeks later, in March of 1989, Marlene packed up her things to head back to L.A., and I packed my things and headed to the Yoshida household. Although Mitsuko and I would become great friends, I learned many years later what she had been saying was, "What are you thinking bringing a *gaijin* to live at the house? Are you nuts?" But he was the man of the house and that was that.

Practice

I became great friends with the Yoshidas over the last 28 years. As you'll see, their decision to let me live with them changed my life in a profound and meaningful way. Consider being a host family for someone coming from overseas—perhaps someone in a homestay situation, perhaps an exchange student. If that isn't feasible, see if there's a support center for immigrants in your area where you can volunteer to teach English. If you're lucky, you can tie this in with the exercise in the previous chapter, and get to know someone from the country you dream of visiting.

Get To—Smile—Support a stranger.

My six-year homestay begins.
Me, Yoshida, Mitsuko, Ataro, and Kenji, 1989.

Our five-story home. I lived on the third
floor. It would be severely damaged in the
1995 Kobe earthquake and torn down.

16. Get To Life in Japan

We don't know what's going to happen next. That is the miracle of life.

Everyday life at the Yoshidas' home included no shoes in the house, sitting on tatami mats on the floor, incredibly simple breakfasts and dinners of rice, fish, and seaweed, and the five- and seven-year-old boys jumping on my bed, laughing at me as I tried to teach them English. The house was an old five-story office building with the fourth and fifth stories converted to their home. For me to move in, they made the third-floor office into a livable space with a bed, camping stove, and employee bathroom. It worked for me.

It was a 24/7 (another phrase that didn't exist back then) learning experience. Mitsuko and I did well. For the first few months she cooked me breakfast, lunch, and dinner, but at some point I said I could take care of my own breakfast and lunch. My Japanese slowly improved, and our often-silent meals became more conversational. The kids, Kenji and Ataro, were always bouncing around. One time, I made them peanut-butter-and-honey sandwiches, my childhood favorite. The boys spit it out, and finished lunch eating their seaweed-wrapped rice balls.

In June, after I'd been living there just four months, we agreed to extend my stay another three months. I received a cassette tape from Kathy around that time. Dad and I had already been sending cassette messages back and forth, so it wasn't a surprise to get one from her. I was in my room studying, sometime around mid-afternoon, when the mailman delivered it. I sat on a cushion on my floor, ready for a good listen on my hand-held tape recorder.

"Ted," said the familiar voice . . . a little somber for my liking, "I'm sending this message via cassette because I believe it's the best way to deliver the news . . . Mom has breast cancer, and her chances are not good." This was right after comedian Gilda Radner had died of ovarian cancer, which was big in the news. Alone, and lonely, not knowing what to do, I went upstairs and found Mitsuko in the kitchen.

"Mitsuko," I said, "Mom has breast cancer, and—" I was sniffling and tearing up "—it's not looking good." I started to cry. Anticipating a hug, I looked up—and she was gone. She had left the room. *What the—?* It was a sharp lesson in Japanese culture: They don't shake hands, they bow. They don't hug, they walk away. And grown men DO NOT cry. I stood there in shock, then went back to my room and cried to Kathy in a return cassette-tape reply. From then on, I spoke to Mitsuko about Mom's cancer only if I knew I could do it without losing my shit.

The family and I got into a nice routine, and the three-month home stay, free in exchange for teaching the kids English one hour a week, turned into six years. I used the incredibly clean and efficient subways to get around, but mostly I rode a cheap bicycle, with a basket on front, all over the city, in the sweltering-hot summers, the cold winters, and, umbrella in hand, during the late-spring rainy season. I joined two guys I had met in a Japanese-language class I was taking, Andrew from Colorado and Eric from Buenos Aires, on a wild, two-week road trip in a dilapidated Toyota driven by a chain-smoking Japanese kid, to southern Japan. We traveled to Hiroshima and sat at the Genbaku Dome, the epicenter of where the atom bomb was dropped—and I sat on a bench and cried. I did the same thing in Nagasaki. The museums with photos and videos showing the devastation and suffering were heart wrenching. How could humans do that? I wondered. I climbed the symbol of Japan, the 12,000 foot Mt. Fuji, a barren, cone-shaped mountain in the center of the country, and slept on the crater rim in a sleeping bag. It was August 12, 1989, and there was a full moon above and, within billowing clouds, a lightning storm below—while snow swirled up around me. A few years later I skied the Olympic runs of Nagano.

Up the street from our house was a vegetable stand, basically a couple of tables set up on the street under a weathered awning in front of an apartment building. The owner, a man maybe 70 years old with a peg leg, limped around the tables putting vegetables in plastic bags for customers. The first time I visited him he said, in broken English, "You American?"

"*Ohio*. Yes, I am." I replied.

He said something in Japanese I didn't understand as he put a head of cauliflower and other things I had pointed to in the bag. As I pulled out money to pay, he said, "No, no, no, you take, no problem."

"Huh?" I said, "I don't understand."

He then told me that he was honored to have me there, because, atomic bombs aside, the Americans came in at the end of the war in 1945 and were nice and gave out chocolate. If the Russians had come in (after the war they had taken over some of the northern islands of Japan), it would have been a nightmare. Instead, there was little retribution on the Japanese by the American forces, and peace and prosperity were quickly restored. Over the years I would come to learn (since I didn't pay attention in high school) of the horrors inflicted by the Japanese in Asia, and I would wonder what part this man may have had in that. But at that time I just was happy to get the free stuff, which he often gave me when I came by.

Here's another life-changing Get To moment that, much like learning the language, has defined my life ever since: At 10 o'clock one night about five months into the homestay, Yoshida knocked on my bedroom door, looked at me, and said, "We do big business." Yoshida owned a small electronics import-export company.

I said, "Sure, let's do big business." Whatever that meant.

He came in, sat down (on a cushion on the floor, of course), and handed me a small, ripped piece of paper with a phone number on it. He said, "I use James Dean on T-shirts. You call number."

Huh? But whatever. So I picked up the phone, dialed the number, and someone answered.

I said, "Hi there. My name is Ted, and I'm here in Japan with a guy who wants to use a photo of James Dean on T-shirts. He gave me this number to call. Can you help?"

The guy on the other end of the line said, "Sure, my name is Marcus Winslow, I'm James's cousin. How much do you think you're going to sell?"

In my better (but still terrible) Japanese I asked Yoshida. He told me, and I said to Marcus, "About $100,000 in sales."

"Okay," Marcus replied, "Pay me 10% of that, which is called a royalty by the way, and I'll send you some photos to use. I'll have my agent send you a contract tomorrow." And that's how it started.

His agents, Beth and Mark, were godsends, especially Beth, who taught me the ins and outs of "licensing"—the business of taking names, images, and logos, and putting them on products to sell. The contract came via fax that rolled up as it came out of the machine, which I then had to tear into separate pages with a ruler. Yoshida signed it and we sent it back to Marcus with a check for $10,000. A week later an envelope arrived with photos of James Dean. Yoshida's company, Sunworld, started selling James Dean T-shirts.

A month later, Yoshida stopped by my room again and said, "Call him back. We want to make baseball caps." James Dean baseball caps? Really? So I did, and for an extra $3,000, we added baseball caps to the contract. So it went: every few weeks Yoshida would stop by, I would call Beth, and we would add more product to the contract. Although still bartending, I started working a couple of days a week at Yoshida's office in the city facilitating the communications.

Yoshida at one point stopped by a desk I had now been given, looked at the pile of papers all splayed on top, and stated simply, "You file." I filed, setting up a rinky-dink system of tracking the contracts and other things I was doing. I had a typewriter to type letters—and lots of whiteout. I got a book on typing and learned how. And you know what happened? Over the next five years, while I was still bartending, teaching English, and otherwise having a Get To life in Japan, Sunworld sold more than $80 million in James Dean products: shirts, hats, shoes, sunglasses, bags, socks, towels, ski-boot tote bags, and a myriad of other things. We paid Marcus over $4 million in royalties. This unfolding of life, we just don't know. What I do know is that I was having a blast.

Practice

Over the years, I would visit my family in Columbus, and then, often with my Dad, drive the three hours over to Indianapolis, Indiana, to visit Beth and Marcus. He was incredibly humble, and grateful for the windfall of money we generated for him. Watch a James Dean movie. My recommendation is *Rebel Without a Cause*.

Get To—Smile—Experience James Dean.

Bartending at the Wild West Club,
Osaka, 1989. Yeah, I'm a sheriff.

With the gang at
the Wild West Club, Osaka, 1990.

17. Get To Build an Empire (Part 1)

It often looks like everyone else is so natural in business. But even Steve Jobs just figured it out one day at a time in his garage. That, and a little luck, is all you need to make it work, one day at a time. Of course, genius is genius, I'm not taking that away from Steve.

About two years into the James Dean program, in 1991, Yoshida asked me to call Pepsi-Cola in New York. So I did.

"Hello," I said. "I'm with someone here in Japan who wants to use the Pepsi-Cola logo on product." The guy on the other end of the line, Don Roach, said that he'd be in Japan in a few weeks to interview other companies that were also interested in the rights to use the Pepsi name. I said, "Great, thanks for also meeting with us while you're here."

Don was coming to Japan to meet with some of the largest companies in the world: Dentsu, Marubeni, Hakuhodo. All multi-billion-dollar firms. That our little five-person company (six if you include me, but I was just a part-time "translating bartender") was getting a meeting with this Pepsi exec was a big deal. Before he arrived, I sent him a fax offering to pick him up at the Osaka airport. I assumed one of the other companies had set up a limo, but thought I'd offer. They hadn't. So on a Monday a few weeks later, one of my colleagues and I headed to the airport and met him. It was morning and we were able to bring him back to the office for our meeting. I was about to present a plan to this Pepsi exec on selling Pepsi merchandise in Japan. This was no small deal, especially when you consider that we were still selling just a handful of James Dean things. We were projecting $50 million in sales of Pepsi product.

Don walked into the small, second-floor lobby / meeting area in our building and, as he looked over at the piano, drums and guitars that were set up, exclaimed, "No way!" I explained to him that Yoshida loved music as a hobby, and I'd played drums in high school, and that we sometimes jammed.

Don put his bag down there on the spot, walked over, sat at the piano and started a medley of Beatles songs. I looked at Yoshida, who had joined us (but hadn't even been introduced to Don yet). We smiled and I walked to the drums while Yoshida picked up the bass guitar, and we commenced an hour-long jam session. The head of sales was on guitar, and one of the other guys grabbed a tambourine. Totally wild.

After the jam, during which we laughed and I sang "Well— she was just 17, and you know what I mean . . . ," we sat down to talk business. We met for a couple of hours, showed him some James Dean product samples, and made a presentation of what we would do with the Pepsi brand. Of course, Pepsi the drink was not part of the contract because it's been sold in Japan since the end of WWII. But it was a pretty impressive plan (by our standards, anyway), with mock-ups of baseball caps, T-shirts, keychains, and other products with the Pepsi logo. He was cordial and thanked us, saying that his week was full of meetings and he'd get back to us.

As he walked out, knowing he was on his way to meet all of those multi-national firms, I knew we weren't going to get the account. But I smiled and softly sang to myself, "When I find myself in times of trouble, Mother Mary comes to me, speaking words of wisdom, let it be . . ."

On Thursday afternoon Don called and asked if he could stop by to see us the following day. "Of course, come on over," I replied. He walked in at about noon and headed right for the piano. We didn't hesitate—we almost ran to our respective instruments and started to jam again. When we were finished, sweaty and laughing, we all sat at a table and I said, "So how was it this week?" Don replied, "You know, I met some pretty impressive companies, with some pretty impressive people. But I'm tired of the big guys getting all the breaks. I'm awarding you the exclusive contract for Pepsi-Cola licensing in Japan."

Are you kidding me? Did we really know what that meant? In the end, over a five-year period starting in 1991, contracting with more than 50 companies producing hundreds of styles of products with the Pepsi logo, we generated over $500 million in sales. I wondered about fate, or luck, in having learned to play the drums in high school all those years before. Don and I became great friends and played a lot of music together. Using the money he made from our sales, he retired in 2010 at the age of 70 to a life of sailing. He died two years later of a heart attack while at the helm of his small sailboat in Sydney Harbor.

Practice

Think of something you want to create and sell, and imagine selling it in an online store. Maybe it's a line of T-shirts you've thought of selling on Etsy, or a new kind of window screen. (Remember my portable screen door that someone else ultimately succeeded with?) Do one thing toward creating that product: look up the rules for selling on Etsy or Cafe Press or Amazon; have lunch with a friend who has the technical know-how to help you make that window screen; write an outline of the novel you've dreamed of self-publishing.

One guy you may have heard of, Frank Kern, started by selling a *Teach Your Parrot to Talk* book online, and turned it into a multi-million-dollar business. Granted, Frank is a marketing guru, but still, he sold a book about teaching parrots to talk and created an empire.

Get To—Smile—Start a business,
create an empire!

18. Get To Olympics

My dad called me a jack of all trades, master of none. But whether mastering a few things, or dabbling in many, do what you love as often as you can. That's all that matters.

As I was slowly building the business with Yoshida and the Sunworld guys, I continued to study both Spanish and Japanese. Although still attending the Japanese school where I had met Andrew and Eric, I wanted more intense and personal study. The local *gaijin* magazine, *Kansai Timeout*, had ads for Japanese teachers, and through one of these I met a wonderful woman named Saito, who I simply called "Sensei," the honorific term for "teacher."

Sensei was a widow who lived by herself in a quiet house on the outskirts of Osaka. I made the 30-minute bike ride from my home three mornings a week for a two-hour lesson. Her father had been a high-ranking general in the Japanese army during the war, stationed in China where she was born. When the war ended, he was sentenced to a work camp in Mongolia and died, and she was shipped back to Japan. She told me a story of how, on the boat home, she heard an explosion and looked out to see that a ship accompanying theirs had hit a mine, and she watched it sink. I didn't ask, but in the silence after she finished telling it even I could hear the screaming people.

After a normal childhood, she married, but her husband died of a heart attack when she was 39, leaving her to raise her three kids alone. By the time I met her she was 55 and living a peaceful, Buddhist-like existence in her tranquil home. I continued to ride my bike to her house every week that I was in Japan for more than six years. Did I mention the sweltering summers, freezing winters, and downpours of the spring rainy season? We would drink tea, snack on seaweed and rice balls, talk, and study. These days, when people say, "Wow, you speak Japanese," I reply, "If you drink a lot of green tea, eat seaweed, and talk and study a lot, you too can learn Japanese." At the same time, I don't take it for granted that I got to do that, and I'm grateful beyond measure that this experience was available to me.

Soon after Marlene left, I met a great lady who was originally from Barcelona, Montse Mari, who owned a Spanish Cultural School in central Osaka. I enrolled and began taking Spanish lessons in the evenings. My Olympic fantasy still blossomed in front of me, and 1992 was fast approaching. In 1990, telling Yoshida I just had to follow my dream, I went to Barcelona for a three-month Spanish immersion program. If I was going to translate for the Olympics there was work to do! It was phenomenal, as I became more fluent in the language and fell in love with that city. I returned to Japan to continue my studies, bartend, and work with Yoshida—and then in 1992, my dream of going to Barcelona to translate for the Olympics came true! NOT. Three weeks before the Olympics, which began on July 25, I went to Barcelona, rented a room, and proceeded to look for work. Who was I kidding? I could still barely speak Japanese, and my Spanish was conversational at best. Besides, with the Gulf War happening, the Japanese had decided to stay home so there was no one to translate for.

But as luck (or angels?) would have it, I had become good friends with a Japanese woman in my Spanish immersion class, Machiko, whose husband was the head of the Japan Travel Bureau (JTB) in Barcelona. Machiko told me that there were hundreds of tickets to the Olympic games available because the Japanese didn't come. She said, in either Spanish or Japanese (I don't remember), "And the tickets are free!" Get out! So every morning we walked into the JTB office, riffled through a shoebox of tickets, picked the events for the day, and "did" the Olympics for the full two weeks. From the opening ceremony (remember the archer shooting the flaming arrow hundreds of feet up to light the Olympic torch towering over the stadium?) to the closing ceremonies—to the U.S. basketball Dream Team (they trounced Spain, but the sold-out crowd of raucous Spaniards loved that they were even playing against the Americans and were as rowdy and as happy as could be)—to gymnastics and swimming and every event in between.

One day Elton John, one of my favorite artists ever, was playing at the 15,000-seat Barcelona Football Stadium. Machiko and I bought two tickets and headed over. There were thousands of people waiting outside the front gates. Since it was a festival event with no assigned seats, many people had, like us, arrived early. We decided not to wait, accepting our fate of seats way in the nosebleed section, and went for lunch.

On our return, we were walking on a back street behind the stadium and noticed a group of 20 or so people milling around a gate. I asked what was happening and a guy told us this was a separate entrance for seats at the top. By this time, we were sure the stadium was full, so we decided to wait there instead of walking all the way around to the front (it's a big stadium). Within a few minutes, a guy unlocked the gates and we strolled in. There was a ramp that crisscrossed back and forth up the stadium's back wall. Up and up we climbed. As we got to the top I noticed it was eerily quiet. We walked through an archway leading into the massive structure and into the top rows of seats. And there was—no one. Spread out in front of us, the huge soccer field with a gigantic stage at one end . . . and *no one was there!* The front gates had not been opened. It was like a dream. We were ecstatic and almost ran down the steps between the bleachers and onto the field, and ended up sitting right at the front of the stage in the center. We had front-row seats at the Elton John concert at the Barcelona Olympics.

In the end, I didn't make any money, but I *Got To—Smile—Do the Olympics!*

Along with having an incredibly fun time, I learned a lot about life through meeting with hundreds of diverse people over those several months. The biggest learning experience, and a reminder of finding compassion, happened right at the end.

Sitting on the plane at the gate at the Barcelona airport, I was thinking about my life in general when an older couple came down the aisle and scooted by me to the window and middle seat. My flight back to Japan was via Rome, and my curiosity as to whether they were Spanish or Italian was settled when the woman said, *"Hola. ¿Como Esta?"* I said, in my now-pretty-good Spanish, *"Muy bien, gracias, ¿y usted?"* We chatted a bit during taxi and picked up again after takeoff. They were from Seville, a city in southern Spain, which was hosting the 1992 World's Fair from April to October. They had come up to Barcelona for a few days of Olympics before heading to Italy on vacation. They were quite proud (a nice way of saying judgmental) speaking of how much better Seville was handling their event than Barcelona was handling theirs—although, admittedly, as the Olympics were taking place in Spain, the event was, from their viewpoint, one of the best Olympics ever held.

The woman said, "And what about those stupid Americans, they're all so rude as they walk around our cities so boisterously." I was taken aback and looked at her for a long few seconds. I couldn't swallow. What do I say to that? And then it hit me: Of course, we're heading to Rome and with my broken Spanish, they think I'm Italian. I had learned during my bartending days that to get the best perspective from anyone, to allow them to talk freely, just agree with whatever belief they're speaking about. I decided to play along—and besides, I could stick it to them when we landed.

I said, "Yes, they are a bit rude, but they did get 108 medals, second only to the Soviet Union's Unified Team of 111, at the games. And they did a pretty good job of getting the Iraq army out of Kuwait in the Gulf War, right?"

"Maybe," she said, "but their quest for oil is pathetic." I didn't totally disagree so stayed silent on that point.

The subject quickly shifted to our lives, me telling them I was heading back to Japan where I was studying and doing business. They told me a bit about their kids, about how they wished one had been this or that, and that another had not turned out so good really. I wondered if they even had a relationship with them. They said that after a long and arduous life, they were retired and finally going out to see the world. Their serious and drawn faces told me there was more to the story than they would share with a stranger on a plane. Maybe they didn't share it with anyone. Sitting quietly with them as our conversation faded, I could feel their life, filled with ups and downs and, probably because of their judging and self-righteousness, more suffering than joy. Of course, I didn't know anything about them really, except that, like me, they were just trying to figure it all out with what they had.

When we landed I simply said, *"Adios."* I wasn't so much feeling like sticking it to them.

· · · ·

Saito Sensei and I remained close friends through the years, even after I left Japan. She became senile and died several years ago. I visited her in the nursing home during my visits to Osaka, and on my last visit, when she saw me, she could only just smile. I smiled back, held her bony, wrinkled hand, the translucent skin barely hanging on, and sat with her for several hours, thinking about my passing life. I wondered why we take it all so seriously, and then I smiled, thinking, *We get to do that, too.*

Practice

Make a list of hobbies you've wanted to do in life, things like playing an instrument, learning a language, mastering the Rubik's cube, writing a book, taking voice lessons, etc. Choose one. Now make a list of 12 steps you can take to learn that skill. On the first of each month, commit to doing one of those steps for the next 30 days. After a year, you will have improved tremendously.

Get To—Smile—Follow your dreams.

Barcelona Olympics with Machiko
and her daughter, Ai Chan, July 1992.

Front row for Elton John,
Barcelona Olympics, 1992.

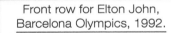

Saito Sensei's home, Osaka, 1993.

19. Get To Build an Empire (Part 2)

Success is being present in the moment—and smiling.

In March of 1994, now becoming more fluent in Japanese, I was introduced to Jonathan Zilli, a Senior Vice President of Paramount Pictures. We set a meeting in the lobby of a London hotel, and when we met he said, "Call me JZ." I thought, *I'm a bartender and I get to call a movie studio executive JZ. How cool is that?*

He said, "I heard you've been doing licensing for Pepsi Cola in Japan."

"Yes," I said tentatively, "and?"

"Well, we own the movies *Star Trek*, *Top Gun*, *The Godfather*, and most of the Audrey Hepburn films such as *Roman Holiday*, *Sabrina*, and *Breakfast at Tiffany's*. Could you guys sell stuff with those movie images on them?"

I didn't think so, but I said, "Of course."

I returned to Japan, and a faxed contract appointing us as the "agent" for Paramount Pictures in Japan soon arrived. By this time Yoshida and the guys were pretty good at putting James Dean's face and the Pepsi logo on things, but they had no idea what to do with a movie title. At first they were excited, putting a picture of Tom Cruise from the movie *Top Gun* on a T-shirt to sell, but when Norman, the Paramount attorney, saw it, he freaked out. The fax from Paramount's legal department was clear: "You can't use Tom Cruise's image on products!"

Enter Sunamori, a friend of Yoshida's who was renting a desk in our building and had his own marketing company. Sunamori said he could do some deals, even without Tom Cruise or other actor images. A month later he came into the office and said, "Hey, I got a deal from a company that wants to turn *Roman Holiday*"—the 1953 film that won a number of Academy Awards, including Best Actress for Audrey Hepburn—"into a stage play."

"Wow," I said, "that's cool. How much will they pay for the right to do that?"

"A million dollars!"

What? So I began negotiating a million-dollar deal for a Broadway-type stage play in Tokyo. It was a two-year negotiation (negotiating with the Japanese is a story unto itself), but in the end the play was a huge success in Japan, generating millions of dollars to Paramount in rights royalties. It was time to quit my bartending job.

Given our success with Paramount, many studios began calling me asking if we would represent their films, TV shows, or artists, and for the next 15 years we did. Yoshida's Sunworld company focused on Pepsi, New Balance, James Dean, and other "brands"; meanwhile, until his crash and burn (a tragic tale I'll share shortly), Sunamori's division of Sunworld, Sun R & P, focused on entertainment. We became the agent for Sony Pictures and Sony Music, including the films *Ghostbusters*, *Men in Black*, and *Spider Man*, the classic TV library with *Bewitched* and *I Dream of Jeannie*, and music-artist greats such as Mariah Carey, Celine Dion, Kiss, and Michael Jackson. We represented MGM Studios and their films *Pink Panther*, *Rocky*, *Great Escape*, and *Robo Cop*; 20th Century Fox's TV shows *24* and *The Simpsons*, as well as their films *Avatar, Alien,* and *Planet of the Apes*; CBS's *Star Trek*; and DreamWorks' *Shrek* and *Kung Fu Panda*. We did deals for Hollywood-themed arcades, stage plays for *Rain Man, Ghost,* and *Zorro*, a cosmetic line for Audrey Hepburn, an apparel line for Grace Kelly, the Bruce Lee attraction I had gone to visit when Dad died, and multimillion-dollar *pachinko* deals (*pachinko* are slot machines in Japan) for dozens of films. Over the years, the projects Sunworld did generated hundreds of millions of dollars in product sales in Japan.

You'll forgive me if in this instance I don't use *Get To— Smile—Do it!* but simply say: What the fuck? This life is so crazy! And it was about to get crazier. By the way, people were starting to make fun of my Osaka-ben—and I was in heaven!

Practice

Buy one lottery ticket. The payout has to be over $100 million, and the drawing at least three days away. Keep the ticket in your pocket and look at it several times a day. Spend those days imagining what you would do if you won. When they draw the numbers and you don't win, realize the joy you received for that dollar.

Get To—Smile—Dream!

Never do this exercise more than once a month lest you become dependent on luck for your success.

The musical *Roman Holiday*, opening night, Tokyo, Japan, 1998.
Assistant to Sunamori, Sunamori, me, Yoshida, Roupen
(Paramount Pictures), actress Mao Daiichi, JZ (Paramount Pictures).

20. Get To Enlightenment

A glorious jog yesterday. My body was
flowing through or with consciousness.
We were one. There was no limit.
—*Journal entry, Osaka, February 9, 1992*

On February 1, 1992—back before Sunworld took off like crazy, and several months before I headed to the Olympics—something profound happened to me. Or I had a profound experience that was waiting to happen. I'm not sure how to put it, really, but in short—I got to experience enlightenment.

To be clear, I'm not enlightened. Far from it. But I did experience, if only momentarily, the sensation I believe enlightened people have all the time. It was a cool summer morning, 6 a.m., the city just waking up, the rising sun rising (the Rising Sun of Japan, get it?) and softly lighting the sky a pale pink, and I was on a jog through Osaka Castle Park with Andrew. We had become good friends after our Hiroshima road trip and often ran together. As we were crossing a stone bridge over a moat, with the huge, ancient (and many times burned and rebuilt) castle looming in front of us, I was complaining that my Japanese girlfriend had moved to the mountains of Nagoya, a 12-hour bus ride from me, and I was horny as hell without her. He didn't look at me, he just simply said, "Dude, it's all in your mind." The next step I took, I walked into a light, into an understanding that it really *is* all "in my mind." There are so many quotes by great sages and holy people throughout the ages, and regular people in modern times, that have had the same experience:

Last night I lost the world, and gained the universe.
— C JoyBell C.

The sea is only the embodiment of a supernatural and wonderful existence. It is nothing but love and emotion; it is the "Living Infinite." —Jules Verne

I was stunned. We kept running and I said, "Dude, I am god. It's all perfect. It's all in my mind and my mind is not real."

Andrew said, "What the hell are you talking about?"

Everything was amazing. It was glorious. As I mentioned earlier, it was a "pop over the edge into that vast oneness with everything" feeling. We returned home and I washed my hands for 15 minutes, one with the water flowing out over my skin. One with everything. My mind was silent. The Universe, in that moment, was perfect.

When I explain any of this to people even today, I often hear a response like Andrew's ("What the hell are you talking about?") or get a blank stare. But what can I say? That was the experience I was having. A crack in my consciousness—which had begun 13 years earlier when a face-bloodied friend said "Everything happens for a reason"—had split wide open. Over the next several days I scoured bookstores for anything on "spirituality," "enlightenment," and "meditation." In the limited sections with English-language books I found Alan Watts, Krishnamurti, D.T. Suzuki, and of course, Buddha, since Buddhism is one of the two major religions in Japan (Shinto being the other). I had read earlier in my life that the Buddha had attained enlightenment, and since I was feeling something like that, it seemed like a good place to start.

I found my way to the International Zen Temple in the mountains of Hiroshima (Zen is one of several schools of Buddhism). This was a traditional temple, not easily accessible by outsiders. At the time, it was one of the few Buddhist temples in Japan that allowed foreigners to enter and practice meditation.

My first trip, soon after my "awakening," was for ten days. There were a dozen or so other Westerners and a few Japanese. We woke up at 3 a.m. and meditated for two hours, then cleaned the temple in silence, me with a toothbrush scrubbing the bathroom floors. To me, in that state of mind it was heaven. At 6 a.m. we ate (sitting on the floor in silence) a traditional Buddhist meal of rice and vegetables. I was so present, just doing these things. At one point during a meditation, a mosquito landed on my nose. Now, in meditation, you're not supposed to move. So I just sat there, peaceful and quiet, watching cross-eyed as the bug sucked my blood. It was transformational to experience that way of being, as opposed to slapping the fucker dead.

After breakfast, we went out to the fields and planted or harvested vegetables. I loved digging from the dirt with my hands the bamboo shoots that we would have for dinner in the evening. In the afternoons we lazed around, reading books, studying Japanese and listening to the locusts in the warm summer stillness. Blissful. At night after a dinner of rice gruel and vegetables from the garden, we'd have another two-hour mediation, and then a discourse with the monks, discussing the nature of life and enlightenment. I was in such a Get To mentality, totally in love with life.

It was here that I met Nick.

Practice

Plant something in your garden. If you don't have a garden, buy a pot, some soil, and some seeds. Put your hands in the dirt and feel the soil. Raise your palms to your face and be filled with the earthy scent. Feel the cold tap in your hand as you turn on the water to fill your watering container, and listen to the sounds of the water change, like musical notes, as it flows from the spout and fills it up. The warmth on your skin as you step outside to water your plant; the sound of traffic, close or far, early or later in the day.

Then, every day for 30 days, set a timer for five minutes and sit with your garden, watch the plants emerge.

Get To—Smile—Life unfolding!

21. Get To Hang with Bon Jovi

Regular people and famous people are all just—people. Like most of us, they are just trying to experience happiness in their lives.

I've negotiated hundreds of deals over the years, all fascinating and unique in their own right. But my favorite was the *pachinko* (slot machine) we did for the band Bon Jovi. In 2005 a Japanese company called and said they wanted to make a Bon Jovi machine to sell in Japan and asked if I could help. A number of years prior, I had met Jon Bon Jovi's cousin, Joseph, while I was working with Sony Pictures and Sony Music. Although we never hung out or anything, during the little time we did connect he was a really good guy and was easy to rap with. So I found his number and gave him a call.

"Hey," I said. "You think your cousin would go for a million bucks to do a slot machine in Japan?"

"Never hurts to ask," he said. A few days later Joseph called back, telling me that Jon had agreed and that he, Joseph, would handle the contract on behalf of the band. Over the next several months, we negotiated back and forth, and finalized the deal.

The Japanese firm started production, which included newly made animation of the band that would be shown on a little screen in the middle of the machine. In 2006, the band did a tour in Tokyo, and we set up a meet-and-greet after the concert for the president of the company. Before the concert, Joseph introduced me to Jon for the first time. He was cordial, but cool, to the point of being a bit of a dick. Here I'd brought him a $1 million deal, and he's a dick to me? *Fucker*, I thought.

After the concert, the company president, his wife, and a handful of staff, along with Sunamori and some of our staff, found ourselves in some cleaned-up-for-meet-and-greet storage room in the bowels of the humongous 55,000-seat Tokyo Dome. There was some quiet talking and anticipation as we waited for Jon and the band. Thirty minutes later they strode into the room. Everyone swooned. Can I be honest? I swooned. We had just watched these four men perform on stage for two hours, playing songs they wrote that are a permanent part of our culture: "Livin' On a Prayer," "Wanted Dead or Alive," "You Give Love a Bad Name." Don't get me wrong, I'm a Zeppelin/Stones kind of guy, not this '80s pop shit—but it was powerful and thrilling to be in person with them. *Maybe he's a dick*, I thought, *but Jon is a true rock star.* There I was, standing between Jon Bon Jovi and the president of this billion-dollar company, translating. I was getting to do that? Jon lightened up and smiled a lot. It was really fun and the band signed a few shirts and posters and hugged a few of the almost-fainting women. Everyone was happy and we all looked forward to getting the slot machine finalized.

About a year later, in 2007, Bon Jovi headed over to Tokyo for another series of sold-out concerts. This time, we arranged that the company would set up the now-completed machines in a suite at the Park Hyatt where the band was staying. (The Park Hyatt was where the movie *Lost in Translation* was filmed. Spot-on movie about Japan, by the way!) The idea was to have the band come to the suite and test the machines and approve the designs.

To make that happen, along with arranging the suite, Joseph and I had the Japanese company pay for our trip to Japan, including rooms at the Hyatt. The band rented out an entire floor, and naturally we stayed on that floor. We arrived at the hotel mid-afternoon and Joseph said, "The band will meet at the Group Room at 6 p.m. to head to dinner. See you there." The Group Room is a hotel suite with the door propped open, filled with food and drinks—a place where the band and roadies gather to hang out, usually during the jet-lagged middle of the night. *Cool,* I thought and headed off to get some work done in my room.

At 6 p.m. I headed over to "the room" and the band and a few of the crew were standing there. As I walked up, Joseph said, "Hey guys, you remember Ted, who put this deal together and translated at the concert last year."

Jon got the biggest smile on his face and said, "Of course! Hey Ted, how's it going?" Richie, Dave, and Tico said the equivalent of "Hey bud, what's happenin'?"—and just like that I was part of the group. We went down the back elevators to the waiting limos and headed to dinner. At the restaurant, there were a dozen or so tables for the band and crew. I sat with Jon, Richie, Joseph, and a violin player who was touring with the band at the time. It was light and easy, and we talked about life, about touring. Jon and Richie talked about their teenage kids. I talked about my life in Japan. I smiled, thinking of how I had judged Jon. I thought, yet again, *Who am I to judge anyone, ever?* It's not like we became best friends, but I did find that Jon is a really great guy. Engaging, fun to talk with, and in the end, like all of us, just trying to figure this whole thing out.

We all went back to the hotel for drinks and hung out chatting until 2 a.m. Two days later I rode in the limo with the band after the concert, fans screaming and yelling as we slowly crept through the parking lot. I got to hang out with Bon Jovi.

As promised, the slot-machine company had set up a suite on another floor of the hotel with all the machines displayed. So the day after our dinner, I helped corral the band, and we all went down to see the machines. I translated for the three Japanese guys making the presentation on how the machines worked, and the band loved them! What's really cool is that they especially loved the animation that played on the screen in the middle of the slot machine. In the midst of the excitement Sunamori said, "Hey Jon, we'll use that animation and make a kid's TV show." Jon replied, "Great, I look forward to it." (This is yet another story for another time, but, in short, a year later Sunamori and I sat in a London hotel board room presenting *Bon Jovi: The Animated Series* TV show to Jon and his attorneys.)

Sunamori had arranged a party that evening in the suite they used for the afternoon presentation. There were a lot of girls and a lot of alcohol. By the time we arrived, it started to get really crazy. I don't know where they all came from, but I heard later it was some Japanese kink club (what that is, and how Sunamori knew about it, I never found out). There were naked Japanese women and people having sex on the floor in the main room and other rooms in the suite. There was even some sadomasochist thing with one woman tied up on the floor naked and getting whipped by a guy. It was weird—and wild. Now, I got to experience that, and although I would love to say something gossipy about how Jon was all drunk and with a bunch of Japanese women, I can't. He and I sat off to the side with the other guys, laughing and talking but otherwise staying out of the fray. It was like we were in a movie. Maybe I would have joined when I was a kid and unmarried? But I guess we're all getting older.

What was really fun was at one point Jon looked at me and said, "Ted, tell everyone they get tickets to the concert tomorrow night!"

No way, 25 tickets to a sold-out Tokyo Dome show? That was cool! What is even cooler, the next night when everybody arrived at the show, instead of seats way in the back of the arena like I'd assumed, they were 10th row, center. Everyone was amazed and thrilled. I swear I heard the woman who had been tied up say, "This is even better than last night." Of course, the show was powerful. It was a highlight of my get-to life.

A short note about fame. Similar to when I first met Jon, when I met Jack Nicklaus—inarguably the most famous and accomplished golfer in history—he was a dick.

Wait, I have way too much reverence for Mr. Nicklaus to say it like that.

How about, he was *standoffish*.

In 2011 my company became the agent for his apparel brand, Golden Bear, in Japan. I had received a call from Andy, his head of licensing, who asked if I could help oversee the al-ready-established business in Japan.

"Represent Jack Nicklaus's business? Hell yeah!" You see, Jack grew up in Columbus, and although he graduated before I was even born, we went to the same high school, Upper Arlington. Jack is known as the Golden Bear, our high school's mascot. So I felt connected.

When I told Andy the serendipitous nature of this opportunity, he really didn't give a shit. "Can you help me with my business?" is all he wanted to know. Yes, sir.

The Nicklaus company businesses span the globe, from Jack Nicklaus golf clubs, equipment, and apparel, to Jack Nicklaus fashion umbrellas (they sell millions in Korea) and a huge golf-course design business, with Nicklaus-designed courses around the world. Jack often does speaking engagements and also started and runs the prestigious Memorial Golf Tournament in Dublin, Ohio, held yearly during Memorial Day. He's a busy guy, so I didn't deal with him directly.

About a year into our business, there was dinner hosted by the Nicklaus Companies in Florida near their headquarters. Many international business associates of Jack's attended, and I, along with several Japanese colleagues, joined. The restaurant was nice but not over the top (I could have easily bartended there, I thought), and our group of about 40 people were seated in a semi-private area at various tables. As the hors d'oeuvres were being served, Jack and his wife, Barbara, came in. Everyone stood and clapped, and Jack gave a short greeting. He has a very down-home way about him—"humble" is probably the right word. I liked him. The main dishes came, it was a pretty jovial dinner, and I translated for the Japanese with the various other international guests we met. Jack and Barbara sat at a table with some other folks, Jack in a chair at the end and Barbara on a bench seat against the wall. I noticed a place to sit on the bench seat next to them.

Here's my chance, I thought and walked over. I sat down and introduced myself. "Hi, I'm Ted and oversee your Japan business."

Jack formally said, "Nice to meet you," and turned away to talk to the guy on the other side of him.

That's it? Having been through it with Jon and others, I didn't take it so personally this time, but I was still disappointed. Standoffish! Barbara was friendlier, and we chatted about Columbus a bit. At least she was sweet.

Fast-forward nine months. I was back in Florida at the Nicklaus offices meeting with Andy. I had been to the offices before, but Jack hadn't been there. I enjoyed the subdued nature of it, how it smelled like golf. Not grass, *golf*. It's hard to explain. There are long hallways that you want to putt a ball down, and the golf trophies on display and the photos of Jack and all the other great golfers. Wow!

I was sitting with Andy in his office when Jack walked in. Andy said, "Jack, you remember Ted, who heads up Japan for us?"

Jack came over, shook my hand, and said, "Of course, how's it going?"

I said, "Great, I love working with your brand."

He smiled warmly and we were buds, just like that. He told some stories about developing the Muirfield clubhouse and we talked about Columbus. I said, "You know what, I went to Upper Arlington."

"Really? That's great. We left Columbus in '69, but I am a Golden Bear."

I laughed. Then I said, "My grandfather was athletic director of Ohio State. Richard Larkins."

Jack got a huge smile on his face and said, "Dick Larkins? Of course I knew him! He was a great man and helped me a lot during my college years and turning pro." (Jack actually dropped out of Ohio State to turn pro, a big deal in 1961. Ohio State granted him an honorary doctorate in 1972.) We talked and laughed for 45 minutes. We met again at a cocktail reception during the following Memorial Tournament in Dublin, Ohio. I was able to introduce him to Pat and we all chatted about life. Jack Nicklaus, what a great man!

I've met, some briefly but to various degrees, many stars besides Jon and Jack: Celine Dion, Deepak Chopra, Tom Hanks, Mariah Carey, George Takei, Kiefer Sutherland, Gloria Estefan, Akebono (arguably the most famous Sumo wrestler in history), King Abdullah of Jordan, and Barbara Eden *(I Dream of Jeannie)*. I met the guys from Earth, Wind and Fire and, after dancing back-stage during a concert in Osaka, I joined them for a private sushi dinner. What I've found is that fame attracts all kinds of people, good and bad (including kink clubs) to them. The famous have learned to put up a wall to protect themselves. But once there is trust built, they become just regular folks trying to make sense of life and—as I said at the start of this chapter—be happy.

Practice

"WNCI and you're the 10th caller! You just won two tickets to see Led Zeppelin at Richfield Coliseum in Cleveland!" an excited voice on the phone said.

"I won!" I yelled to the empty kitchen. I was home alone and standing next to the yellow phone on the wall after pushing the buttons for the WNCI phone number over and over. After the 20th busy signal, I was about to give up when they answered. "What's your favorite radio station?" he asked. "WNCI!" I said excitedly in my 15-year-old dorkiness. On April 27, 1977, I was going to see Led Zeppelin. My first concert.

The deal I made with Mom was that Rick would join me, but at the last minute he bailed. My now-single-parenting, exhausted, and depressed mom said, "Whatever," and reluctantly allowed me to ride my bicycle five miles that evening to the WNCI radio station, where a bus would drive 25 winners two hours to the concert. The pot-smoking hippies passing joints on that bus, the laser lights cutting through the smoke-filled, 20,000-seat, sold-out arena, the band's incredible, heart-pounding sound, was—overwhelming. I couldn't stop smiling, sitting there, alone but part of something amazing. The three-hour concert was intense. I knew "Stairway to Heaven," but I wasn't prepared for "Black Dog," "Kashmir," and "Nobody's Fault But Mine"—it took my breath away. I smiled the whole time.

Remember your first concert. Who was it? Where was it? Who were you with? What seat? Remember the smells and sounds.

Get To—Smile—First concert!

Translating for Jon and the Bon
Jovi band, backstage, Tokyo Dome, 2006.

With Pat Torrance and Jack Nicklaus,
Memorial Tournament, Columbus, Ohio, 2014.

Hanging with Celine Dion backstage,
Osaka, 1997. Kenji, me, Celine, and Yoshida.

22. Get To Brother Nick

I said, "Meeting you was fate."
He replied, "Or meeting me is just
life, and fate is just another concept
of the mind to explain the
unexplainable?"
—*Conversation with Nick, journal entry,*
Osaka, May, 1992

People come and go in life. Yesterday, a truck plowed into people on a sidewalk in France, killing over 80 people. Gone. Our daughter, Cole Grace, here and gone. Dad, Mom, gone. But Nick is different. He's not gone. Dead, yes, but not gone.

When I first arrived at the temple I noticed a very quiet guy off reading by himself. It was a hot, still afternoon. The smell of the temple incense wafting over the porch overlooking the mountains created such a peaceful feeling. I went up and sat next to him and said, "Hi, I'm Ted."

He slowly looked up, paused, and said simply, "I'm Nick." He had a soft easy smile.

I was comfortable sitting there quietly for a minute before I asked, "What are you reading?"

"It's a Hindi language book." *Oh?* He continued, "I'm on my way to Calcutta to work at Mother Teresa's orphanages. I stopped here in Japan to meditate while I learn Hindi." *Oh.*

Nick was a doctor from Texas, 28 years old and a real free spirit. When I told him about my enlightenment experience he smiled and said, "Cool." That was it, no drama—just, "cool."

We spent the next ten days doing Zen stuff. There were the hours of meditation, morning work in the fields, afternoon naps on futons on the wooden floors, and the other daily rituals of temple life, including the long talks with the monks. But one thing we did, which in hindsight is a bit embarrassing, was called *takuhatsu*. We wore robes, straw shoes, and straw hats and went into the city to collect alms for the temple. We'd stand at the side of the road, completely still, chanting something like, *"Om wa san gan dan, san gyo nan,"* over and over, while holding a basket for people to put money in. I didn't know what I was saying or what it meant, but I thought I was pretty cool. Looking back, a white boy dressed as monk with a crappy accent probably looked pretty silly. But I got to do that . . . and we made some money for the temple.

I returned to Osaka and daily life. The buzz of enlightenment slowly faded, although as time passed I did have occasional "flashbacks" in which I'd have realizations such as "time doesn't exist," "everything is perfect just as it is," and "God is just playing hide and seek with himself, and I'm it." Those things don't make a lot of sense when I look back on them now, but all were amazing moments in their own right.

Nick came to visit. He really was a good guy. Easy to be with and fun. We talked for hours about life and the meaning of existence, told stories from our past. I loved Nick, maybe as the brother that disappeared? He was an old soul, as the spiritual people say, and it felt like I'd known him for years and years. We did some touring around Osaka and the port city of Kobe, talked about nothing and everything, and sat quietly a lot together. Then he was off to India.

Practice

Think about your current best friend and remember how you met. What did you think of them then? What do you imagine they thought of you? And how did those impressions change over time?

Now repeat this exercise, thinking of a different friend.

Get To—Smile—Fateful meetings.

The Osaka Castle where it all began, 1992.

Takuhatsu with the monks and fellow *gaijin*, on our way
to collect alms in the city, March 1992. I'm in the center.

Life with a monk: International Zen Temple,
Hiroshima, Japan, March 1992.
Nick is second from the right; I'm standing in back.

23. Get To India (Part 1)

There appear to be no rules except
survival. Taxis follow no rules. We
ran over a dog last night. It yelped.
I cringed, knowing it could have been
a human.
                    —*Journal Entry, Calcutta, India,*
                                        March 7, 1993

I love India. I know many people who have said they can't stand
the begging, the dirt, the smell, the heat. But for me, although I
was only there for eight days, it was life changing. I "got to"
India. It's in my bones, like I had a second birth. I never looked
at life the same after India. I never took things for granted to the
same degree. If there were ever a moment in time where I fully
experienced the Get To attitude, it was during my trip to India.

Nearly a year after Nick left Japan, so in February 1993, I
received a crazy postcard from him. "Brother Ted, India is an
amazing place. It's like Mars. You wanna come?"

"Hell yeah," I wrote on a return postcard, and told him I'd
see him at the Calcutta airport at 1 p.m. on a Sunday the following month. Easy enough. Busy with life in Japan, I didn't prepare
for my trip. Nick would pick me up and I'd leave it all to him.
Thank God for friends.

I landed in Calcutta on Sunday, March 7, and walking out
of the plane on raggedy stairs down onto the hot, cracked tar-
mac, I thought to myself, *OMG, this is Mars!* I was lucky as I was
the second one off the plane and one of the first in the customs

line—because even then it took 30 minutes to get through. There were ten guys standing there, looking at my passport, talking to each other, laughing, just taking their time. The line in back of me began piling up. *Mars.*

I eventually got through and as I came out to the waiting area, Nick wasn't there. I walked outside and looked around. No Nick. I had a sinking feeling that I was going to get to do this on my own. I didn't have a guide book. No local currency. No idea. No plan. As Scooby Doo would say, "Ruh-roh."

So, first things first. I walked back into the terminal to the money-exchange counter. There were six guys at a table behind it playing cards. They were laughing and smoking, and I could barely see through the haze in the dimly lit room. I said, "Excuse me, can I exchange some money?" One of the guys looked up, smiled and said, "Oh no, we take lunch break. You come back one hour."

I just stood there, and they kept playing cards and smoking and laughing. Eventually, I sat down on an old, weathered wooden bench—and smiled. I wasn't antsy or anxious. I simply waited there, my mind quiet, for an hour. When they finally came back to the counter, it took another 20 minutes to complete the transaction. I smiled. I can't explain why I was okay with it all, but there was something so unique about the experience, something in the slowness of everything around me, that I was just open to what was happening.

Finally, with money in my pocket (I would later learn it was more than most people in India make in years), and my backpack on my back, I headed out to get a taxi. I didn't have any idea where to start (I'd left the postcards with Nick's address back in

Osaka), but I figured at least I could get to the post office in downtown Calcutta, since in many Asian cities they have message boards for foreigners. There was a line of taxis, all old, rickety, and rusty. I approached the first one and said "excuse me" through the window to the napping driver. He was young and rail thin, and, slowly opening his eyes, he said, "Come, come, my friend, get in." I told him where I wanted to go and he smiled and said, "Okay, okay. Post office, okay."

We started driving, slowly traveling on dilapidated roads, weaving around cows. One time, he came to a stop for a cow, lit a cigarette, and waited for it to move. Then slowly we drove on. (In the Hindu religion, cows are sacred.) The landscape of people working in the fields, people walking, people on bicycles, smog-spewing cars, the dirt huts along the way—everything was more than I imagined India to be. This was definitely Mars.

We drove into downtown. It was crowded with rickshaws, motorcycles with four and five people on them, and street vendors of every kind. It smelled so . . . sweet and dirty at the same time. It was hot, and it all wafted through the open windows. At one point we came to a stop in traffic— on railroad tracks. A train was coming. It was slow, but coming, and a train nonetheless, and we weren't moving, bumper to bumper with the car in front and another just behind. I started to panic (no matter how much you "get to" do anything, I learned in that moment that potentially getting hit by a train creates panic). I yelled, "Move, move, move!" The taxi driver was yelling at the cars and honking and the train kept coming. I can still see the train driver, silently screaming through his windshield, blowing his horn, making all kinds of gestures with his hands as the train plowed into the back of the taxi and pushed us along until the back of our car slid off the track. The taxi driver screamed the whole time. Then it was quiet. There we sat. My heart pounded as I watched the train keep going, and then I smiled.

The back fender smashed in, but the car drivable, we finally made it to the main post office and I was able to stick a note on a cork board with big letters NICK on the front, telling him I was in town and looking for him and to leave me a message. I figured I'd find a hotel, come back later and add that information to my note.

I made my way to an area known for hotels where foreigners stayed, called Sudder Street, and found a cheap youth hostel. From there I continued my quest looking for Nick. I made the rounds to all the hotels asking if anyone had seen a guy like him. No. I met a few foreigners and asked if they knew a doctor named Nick. No again. I went back to the post office and edited my note.

I knew he was working for Mother Teresa, so I asked the front-desk clerk back at the hostel how to get there. He said that the best way was to go with a guide. Mother Teresa's community was large and spread out, with many buildings located in various slums. A lone foreigner was not a safe bet. Not that Calcutta is unsafe. Even today, 25 years later, it is known as one of the safer cities in India. But having a local person would be a definite plus.

As soon as the clerk said, "You need a guide," a guy appeared at my side. Maybe he was sitting there waiting for anyone, but it felt like he materialized out of nowhere—for me. His name was Stanley and he said he'd happily escort me for a few rupees. Stanley was a gentle soul, just so peaceful, with an engraved smile on his face, he was gaunt, tall, brown-skinned with big bright eyes.

"Hello Mr. Ted, I take you to find the friend. We find him okay, Mr. Ted?" How could I say no?

We spent two days walking around Calcutta, going to the various Mother Teresa locations. He took me to his home in the slums. His one room, about 10 feet by 10 feet, housed his family of four. It was stunning. Pots hanging on the walls, clothes arranged in bins. The beds, they told me, were mats they rolled out on the floor and on top of the cabinets for the kids to sleep on. They were gracious and humble. They made me a lunch of nan and some veggies. Carrying a couple of buckets, I walked to the well with his wife to get water. Row after row of huts all along dusty roads. It was hot, loud, and crowded, and I stood out like a sore thumb. But they all were somehow peaceful and didn't pay much attention to me. I got to experience a side of life, a viewpoint, like nothing I'd ever seen. I wondered about my luck, or fate, at being born into a family that, by contrast, had offered me incredible abundance and wealth. I wondered, *Who am I to ever judge anyone less fortunate than I am? Who am I to not have incredible gratitude for the life I have?* Of course, I am Ted. I sometimes judge the hell out of people, and sometimes take my life for granted. But in that moment I experienced the feeling of humble in a profound way.

One day, Stanley and I were sitting on the curb of a busy, bustling street, enjoying the sights and smells of a cool Indian morning, when a guy came wheeling up on a skateboard-type contraption with a pot of chai tea and four cups. Are you ready for an image shift in your mind? "A guy came wheeling up on a skateboard" is one image. "A guy with no legs, using his arms to propel himself along the road, came wheeling up on a skateboard" is another image all together. The chai guy, I came to learn, stayed alive by selling chai, and hanging out at the backs of restaurants eating the scraps of food from the trash. I also found that many of the disfigured, begging children I encountered had had their limbs broken and twisted—or even cut off—when they were young to help them beg more effectively. I met many of them. Stanley kept them from jumping all over me, but I got plenty of hugs. I cried for them some nights. Not only did I get to feel compassion (for them) and gratitude (for my life), but I got to meet some incredible people. In those short two days, Stanley and I became friends. We drank a lot of chai.

On the third day in Calcutta, I was walking down the street near my hotel, smiling at the intense nature of the life around me, when I looked up and coming toward me was Nick. We walked up to each other and he said, "Hey, Brother Ted."

I said, "Hey, Brother Nick." We hugged.

He said, "I thought you were coming in next week." And I laughed.

Practice

There's something about a cup of tea that encourages you to slow down. Coffee on the fly makes sense. But a cup of tea is somehow peaceful (or it is for me). Make a cup of tea, chai if you have it. Sit in a comfortable, quiet place on the floor and, with great appreciation for life, sip the tea.

Get To—Smile—Drink tea.

India, 1993: I had arrived on Mars.

Nick and I hung out with
some village kids in Bodh Gaya.

Stanley and his family in their
one-room house, Calcutta.

24. Get To Meet Mother Teresa

*Nothing is as important as you think
it is, while you're thinking about it.*
—*Daniel Kahneman*

The next day Nick took me to Mother Teresa's home for the dying, called Kalighat. I spent a few days attending to the dying men. They were sick, and at various stages of approaching death. What a reality I was in—and it smelled pretty bad. I've read in books and heard in movies about "the stench of death hanging in the air." Now I had the direct experience of that. It was intense, cleaning out bedpans, changing bandages, spoon feeding these frail, dying human beings. But I got to do that and I looked at it as an honor.

On the third day we went to her orphanage to take care of the children. In Kalighat the dying men were lost. Most had given up hope. Vacant eyes. No smiles. But the children, many of them missing limbs and with all sorts of maladies, were full of joy and wonder at life. They get to live in the miracle of the moment in whatever form it takes. I met one special five-year-old girl with a name I couldn't pronounce, so I called her Cecilia—after the Simon and Garfunkel song. She was sweet and precious and blind. She held my hand and smiled. I played with her for hours and sang to her, "Cecilia, you're breaking my heart . . ."

Nick and I were walking down a gray-walled, dank-smelling stairwell the next day after some time with the kids and ran into Mother coming up the stairs. Nick stopped her and introduced me. "Mother, this is my friend, Ted." he said. She stopped and cupped her hands over mine and said softly, "Bless you, my child." Such sweet words, such presence. It was like she stared into my heart. I was quiet and held her gaze. After a long moment Nick asked if we could have a photo with her and she politely declined, saying she was on her way to the children. That was cool. I watched her continue walking up the stairs and I stood quietly, in awe.

There was a lot of suffering going on there, and I admired what Mother was doing. I've learned since that even though she had millions of dollars in donations, the facilities were dirty, and she chose to allow many in her care to suffer. Her staff glorified the suffering instead of relieving it. I witnessed that and the incredibly filthy conditions first hand. I didn't think about it at the time, but looking back, what a viewpoint. She refused to allow condoms or any birth control, saying pregnancy is the will of God. Even in the case of rape! *Yikes.* But even with this new information, I love Mother. There was a lot of love going on in those slums and she was certainly doing a lot more in life than serving alcohol to over-privileged rich people. Not to dis on my career as a bartender, but in perspective it does make you think. She got to fulfill her life by helping others her way. Amen.

Practice

Think of your favorite spiritual teacher and visualize meeting them. How do you see yourself with them? What questions would you ask? What would you tell them? What would you hope to hear in reply?

Get To—Smile—Guru.

25. Get To India (Part 2)

*Calcutta is a beautiful place. In the
midst of the trash is a soul, a being
called love, that all humans share.*
—*Journal entry, Calcutta, India,
March 8, 1993*

From Calcutta, we took a train to Gaya, and then rode on the roof of an overcrowded, dilapidated, human- and animal-filled bus for 30 minutes to Bodh Gaya, a religious site where Buddha is said to have attained enlightenment under the Bodhi tree. At the train station I had seen a Japanese kid with a James Dean hat on and smiled, recognizing what I had created. But as I was meditating several hours later under that sacred tree (actually, a descendant of the original tree planted in 288 BC), trying not to think, I thought, "Wow, there is so much suffering in the world, and I'm using my resources for the Japanese to wear James Dean hats." I started to question my role on the planet. But often my deep thoughts go only so far, and so I started not thinking about other things. At least I was getting to meditate under the Bodhi Tree! *Oooooommmmmmmm.*

The next day we took another train to the spiritual capital of India, Varanasi, a city located on the Ganges River. Varanasi is known for their cremation *ghats*, where they burn bodies in order for their souls to go to heaven. It's where the sick come to get healed in the holy river, or die and get cremated on the banks. We walked around seeing all of this. It was hot, crowded, all kinds of languages and people crowded on the river bank.

We met a group of Sadhus, monks that live off the land, traveling around the country on foot their entire lives. We sat with them one night and ate hash. I don't know whether the idea was to get stoned or have a religious experience, but I was just going with the flow. Sitting in that circle of gaunt, smiling men, silently passing a chunk of the foul-tasting stuff around, was surreal.

I would put a piece in my mouth, pretend to cough and spit it into my hand so I wouldn't puke. But I got high anyway. They put a red dot on my forehead.

The next morning, I hired a guy to take me in his rowboat across to the other side of the Ganges, probably a quarter-mile wide, with the intention of visiting a remote village on the other side. I asked Nick to come translate, but he said he felt the "Larkins" thing was something I needed to do on my own.

Practice

I've meditated on and off for many years and have found great comfort from it. These days there are some great apps that help you meditate. My favorite is HeadSpace. The guy, his name is Andy, that guides the meditations in the videos seems really cool and real. Periodically, Deepak Chopra and Oprah offer a 21-day meditation for free. I love that.

You can also just do it on your own. Although there are a lot of ideas about meditating, it's really nothing more than sitting quietly with the intention to quiet your mind. Sit and smile without thinking. Easy. At least for a few seconds. Then your mind is off and running. But string a few of those seconds together, and then a few more, and your life changes.

Here's my version: Sit on a cushion on the floor, or in a chair. Set a timer—20 minutes works for me, but again, no rules. If you've never meditated before, maybe start with five minutes in the morning. After a few days, you might find you want to go longer. Begin by breathing in. Breathe out and count *one*. Breathe in. Breathe out and count *two*. Breathe in. Breathe out and count *three*. Continue this up to ten and then start at one again. Repeat. When you catch your mind having thoughts other than counting, smile, and return to counting from one again. Do this until the timer goes off. You will feel more relaxed. Don't get discouraged. Sometimes I sit, set the timer for 20 minutes, start my first counting, get to five . . . and the timer goes off. Shit, I was thinking that whole time? Oh, well, so much for that session. But usually my thoughts quiet considerably and no matter what, I always feel better afterward.

Here's a more modern version I often use, which I call the 10-Minute Get To Meditation: Set a timer for three minutes and state out loud during that three minutes what you get to do that day—or if it's in the evening, what you got to do that day. When the timer goes off, set it again for seven minutes. Close your eyes, softly smile, and in a whisper (or in your mind) repeat, "Get To— Smile—Be here . . . Get To—Smile—Be here . . . Get To—Smile—Be here." As your mind wanders, just bring it back to the mantra. "Get To— Smile—Be here . . . Get To—Smile—Be here." When the timer goes off, slowly open your eyes and spend a minute in wonder at life.

Get To—Smile—Meditate.

The banks of the Ganges River, Varanasi, India.
Where the sick come to get healed,
and the really sick come to die.

Eating hash with the Sadhus, India, 1993.

India, 1993: I helped a Sadhu clean
his laundry in the Ganges River.

Nick selling beads on the
bank of the Ganges River, 1993.

26. Get To Larkins

*How caught up in the game I choose
to get is up to me. It's easy to forget
it's all a game.*
—*Journal entry, Osaka, May 15, 1992*

This is my version of a parable I heard at some point during my time in Japan: A young monk was peacefully walking through the jungle. A tiger appeared and started after him. The young monk ran, laughing, knowing this could be the end. Just as the tiger was about to pounce on him, he was able to grab a vine and start climbing up the side of a cliff. He was half way up, still laughing, when he saw above him another tiger gnawing at the vine at the top of the cliff, the original tiger hungrily waiting below. A moment later, the young monk noticed a red, ripe strawberry growing next to where he was hanging. With a huge smile, he reached out, tenderly took it off the vine, and slowly took a bite.

In 1990, about one year into my homestay, Yoshida came into my room with a paper catalog showing various products; T-shirts, backpacks, socks, hats. The title was LARKINS COLLECTION — CAPTAIN TED & FRIENDS. In the middle of the six-page catalog was a picture of me and some photos of a Captain Ted doll; a stuffed animal in the form of a pirate, eye patch and all. I said, "What's this?" He said, "Let's do big business, we create LARKINS line of product." I said, "Sure, why not?"

A few days later I was telling Dad about it on the phone and he yelled, "Those fuckin' Japs are trying to take advantage of you, Ted. Get a percentage of sales, that's our name!"

"Dad," I replied calmly, "World War II ended 45 years ago. You gotta get over your impression that the Japanese are imperialists still bent on taking over the world. I've been here a year and I promise, they are really a great people."

Regardless, it was Dad speaking, so I went to Yoshida and asked if I could get paid. He said, "Ted, it's a game. I could take the L off and call it Arkins, but I thought you'd like to play." I said, "Okay, but I get a lifetime of samples of Larkins product." We shook hands. It's the best business deal I ever made.

My part in the Larkins brand development was to help build it internationally and to support communications. To start, my job was to take photos of people in various places wearing the Larkins T-shirts. I took dozens of shirts with me on a trip to the U.S., hired a couple of girls to wear them, and photographed them in San Francisco at the Golden Gate Bridge and other areas around the city. I took the shirts down to the beaches of Los Angeles, putting them on storefront mannequins of various hip apparel stores. In exchange, I left a half-dozen shirts, promising to list their store as a seller of Larkins product in magazines in Japan. In the early 1990s, the Japanese were flooding the U.S. (they had recently bought Pebble Beach and Rockefeller Center), and they were a big part of the tourist population in Los Angeles. I did the same in San Diego, Columbus, Tampa, and other cities.

With 30 rolls of film in hand, I returned to Japan, where a couple of Yoshida's guys in the brand-development department incorporated the photos into presentations and then went to various manufacturers and shared the brand image they were creating. Yoshida was really quite brilliant that way, identifying the "American street brand" boom that would hit Japan in the mid-'90s. The Larkins brand was a perfect fit. Those manufacturers of different products signed up to be part of the growing phenomenon called "Larkins."

So there I was, in 1993, on the banks of the Ganges River, with more Larkins T-shirts and my camera, on my way to a remote village in India to take some photos. The guy I hired to take me over in his rickety rowboat looked 75, but could have been 45, with dark leathery skin. Halfway over, he stopped rowing and with cupped hands took a drink from the river—where corpses had floated by and on the banks tens of thousands of people bathed daily. He got to do that. I didn't. When we reached the other side, I asked him to wait for me, all day if necessary, until I came back. I was excited, and scared. This was wild shit I was doing, heading into the complete unknown.

I started walking down a dirt road toward a forest a mile or so off in the distance. I heard there was a small community of Indians living off the land there. As I got closer I noticed a number of huts around a large pit that looked like a large, unlit campfire. As I got closer still, I saw a group of men sitting on the ground near one of the larger huts. They sat watching me as I slowly walked up and said, "Hi, I'm Ted." They stared. "Um, I'm promoting a line of product and I'd like to offer to pay you to model the clothing." Stares. I'm sure they could hear my pounding heart. Then one of the guys got up and walked towards me. I thought, *Should I run or should I hold my ground?* But as he got closer, a big smile came across his face, and he exclaimed, "Welcome Mr. Ted! Come, come." That was it, we were friends.

I took out the shirts and passed them around. They were so excited, trying them on and walking around modeling. I took pictures of them in their huts and carrying their large metal water jugs on their heads. We had some nan and chai. It was a magical afternoon. Laughing and joking around, they showed me their world. They said that healthcare was the biggest problem because it was a long journey to the nearest facility. I said I would come back someday and build them a hospital. It's been on my mind ever since, and writing this now, I'm reinvigorated to go back and do good by my word and build a hospital, or maybe an orphanage. (Maybe, just maybe, that's what this book is about?) In the rowboat back to Varanasi, and on the return trip to Japan, I smiled a lot, thinking about those men, the life they lived in contrast to mine. *Get To—Smile—Appreciate.*

Over the years, as the brand grew in Japan, I received many, many samples that my family loved to show off: Larkins umbrellas, Larkins wallets, Larkins shoes, shirts, and hats. On her visit to Japan, Mom was walking through the Tokyo train station and she saw a young girl carrying a Larkins bag. She literally screamed, "Oh my God, a Larkins bag! Teddy, go tell her you're Ted Larkins!"

I laughed, "Mom, she doesn't care!" In the past I had seen people wearing Larkins product around and had gone up and announced that I was Ted Larkins. They would look at me like I was crazy. I showed them my passport. "Look, really I'm Larkins." Really, they didn't care. Still, it was very exciting.

Recently, I was speaking with a good friend and colleague from Germany, Jo, and told him about Larkins. He asked how much Larkins product had been sold to date. "Oh, in the last 20 years, about $100 million." He looked at me incredulously and said, "If you had gotten just 4% royalty you would have made $4 million!" I smiled. I got to experience my name as a major brand in Japan. I played Yoshida's game and ended up living with him for six years for free (there is no price for that experience), became fluent in Japanese, traveled the world (usually first class), acquired business acumen and bartender-worthy people skills beyond measure. The agreement I made with Yoshida—"all the samples I want, for life"—as I said, it's the best business deal I've ever made.

Practice

One of the most powerful tools in your Get To arsenal is acknowledging the incredible things you get to do each day. I have a physical notebook, but also "Notes" on my computer and phone, and as often as possible, in the morning, I simply write in one of them, "I Get To ..." and then list at least ten things I get to do that day. Get a notebook or journal, and every day, write: I Get To _____ , and fill in the blank with at least ten things. Twenty if you're feeling it. Smile the whole time.

Get To—Smile—Get to!

Even Nick got in on the
Larkins modeling action. Cool shirt.

Modeling Larkins wear,
San Francisco, 1991.

Larkins catalog with
"Captain Ted, the pirate" dolls.

India, 1993: The village where I made friends.

Villagers modeling Larkins clothes.

In the boat to the other side of the Ganges.
He drank the water. I didn't.

27. Get To Visa

If we, as thinking humans, are aware second to second about what's going on around us and in us, we can find peace. It's getting lost and caught up in thought that keeps us trapped.
—*Journal entry, Osaka, Japan, November 1992*

I returned to Japan from India a much better man than before. Now 29, I was even more intrigued and curious about this experience we call life. I sent Stanley a money order for $50 every month for several years. I did make a half-assed attempt to start a "hospital fund" from a percentage of Larkins sales, asking Yoshida if he would donate. He politely declined. In his defense of not giving, and in my defense for not being more persistent, the early '90s economy in Japan was starting to crumble, and for Sunworld, building the Larkins brand and keeping people employed was the priority, not funding a hospital in some Indian village only I had been to.

My ability to even travel to India from Japan so freely was the result of an intense few months two years prior. I had arrived in 1988 on a tourist visa. It was only valid for three months, after which time you had to leave the country. But the beauty was, as long as you left the country you could come right back "as a tourist." So every three months I took off to some cool new city like Seoul, Hong Kong, or Saipan. One time I put a backpack on and hiked through Thailand. I got to ride elephants through the jungles in Chiang Mai, and for 100 Baht ($2) smoked opium on the floor of a hut with a tribal elder in a small village in the mountains of Chiang Rai. It was on the edge of being touristy, but this was 1990, so it was still pretty real—and I got a buzz. Yoshida paid for my trips to Indiana to visit Marcus and Beth to discuss the James Dean program, and along the way I'd visit friends in California or my family in Ohio.

But by the end of the second year, the immigration guys, upon seeing the many stamps in my passport, started questioning my tourist status. They would say, "Are you sure you're not working here?" I would smile and say, *"Ohio.* No sir." But they were catching on. I had friends who'd been denied entry, and once that happened, there was no coming back. Since I was studying the Japanese language full time, I applied for a student visa. That was easy enough, and good for another year. As that visa was coming to an end I started looking for another option. I took up karate and applied for a cultural visa. That, too, was good for a year. (I hated karate—people kicking and punching me is just not my thing. I broke my big toe on some guy's kneecap.) A year later, at the end of 1991, I would not have an option to stay.

The next and obvious choice was to get a work visa. James Dean and Pepsi—and now New Balance—were growing, and Yoshida wanted me to stay. After all, I was the only one who spoke English in the company. The problem was, you needed a four-year college degree, and yours truly didn't have one. But when did I let a silly thing like that stop me? I found a book titled something like "100 of the Best College Degrees by Mail" and flipped through it. Most names I had never heard of, but there was one that stood out: Honolulu University. It was an accredited university and, although I'm not sure who it was accredited by, it was a university offering degrees nonetheless. I didn't give a shit, I just needed a piece of paper saying I had graduated from college. I applied, paid the $1,500 tuition, and started my degree program. The thing about Honolulu University is that they accept "life credits." I had a pilot's license (3 credits); I spoke Japanese and Spanish (12 credits each); I had been in a band, so, music theory (3 credits); real-estate license (3 credits); karate, so phys ed (4 credits). There were some other things, including some "undergrad" courses at Franklin University in Columbus right after high school, but all told, I already had 42 credits and only needed 50 total to graduate. Imagine that. So, working with my Honolulu U counselor, we came up with a program where I would create three theses on various aspects of business, and upon completion, I would have my degree. I spent several months writing papers about international business, business marketing, and business in Japan. Everything was done by mail or fax.

It's quite an accelerated learning approach, but it worked for me. On December 5, 1991, four months after beginning my quest, I received a bachelor's degree in business administration. Not a moment too soon, as my visa was going to expire on December 10th, the date set with immigration for an interview. The school was going to mail the graduation certificate, but it wouldn't make it in time. I sent a fax, asking my counselor to fax back a copy, since it was an integral part of my visa application. By December 9th it still hadn't arrived, and I started to panic. I faxed him again. No reply. I called and got the answering machine. Please, I begged, if I don't get the paper by tomorrow, I'll have to leave Japan for good. It came, rolled up in the fax machine, the morning of my interview. Whew!

The myriad of required documents, and now, degree from Honolulu U in hand, I got on my bicycle and headed to the immigration office in mid-city Osaka. It was cold and rainy and even with my umbrella I arrived soaked. I sat for a while in the gray, lifeless waiting area, smiling nervously. This was a life-transforming meeting. If they denied my application, I would be on a plane back to the U.S. the next day. But even in that moment there was a part of me that was calm. I knew that for so many people sitting in immigration waiting rooms around the world, denial meant being sent back to places of war, starvation, or political persecution. I would go back to either California or Ohio, to friends and family and all kinds of opportunities. I got to sit there and wait.

A middle-aged woman appeared in the doorway and called out, "Larkins San," even though I was the only one in the room. I stood and followed her through a door into the back office, and she indicated for me to sit in a chair in front of a desk where a middle-aged guy in a gray uniform, matching that of the woman, was sitting. I sat, said, *"Ohio gozaimasu"* (the more respectful form of good morning), and handed him my large envelope of papers and my passport.

He smiled, not so warmly, and said, *"Ohio"* (less respectful because he held all the cards.) We chatted a bit as he leafed through my passport. He said, "So many stamps. Have you been working here?"

"No," I lied, "just studying."

He frowned a bit. *Uh oh*. He pulled the thick stack of papers from the envelope and began looking through them, making various "hmmmm" and "ummm" noises at each one. I stayed calm and smiled, until he stopped at the paper copy of the diploma. He stared at it for a long minute. My heart started racing. "Honolulu University?" he questioned. Shit, did he know? Had someone tried this before?

"Yes." I stuttered and cleared my throat, "Is there a problem?" My heart was now pounding.

He said, "My cousin played volleyball for them. It's a great school."

I thought I was going to faint. "Yes, it's a great school," I said, knowing he probably was thinking of the University of Hawaii. But none of that mattered, because ten minutes later he stamped "approved" on my paperwork.

Several months later, now free to come and go as I pleased to Japan, I joined Andrew in Hawaii for his wedding to Mariko, one of the Japanese teachers from the school we had attended. I stopped by Honolulu U to accept my degree in person. *Get To— Smile—Graduate*.

Practice

Put on the song "Imagine," by John Lennon.
Really listen to the words all the way through.

Get To—Smile—Imagine.

Graduation, Honolulu University, 1992.

28. Get To Sunamori

It is what it is.
—*Dad*

Along with Yoshida, Sunamori was another great influence on my life. A few years older than I was, he had his own marketing company and eventually took over the entertainment-licensing business from Yoshida. From that first *Roman Holiday* stage play in 1994 through 2010, he created tens of millions of dollars in licensing deals. I got to be there, as his consultant, to translate and negotiate the contracts with the movie studios and artists all those years. He was creative and always looking for unique ideas to turn into money. Along with the Bon Jovi slot machine, he created some incredibly powerful programs, including a Pink Panther store at Universal Studios Japan, dozens of TV commercials using clips from famous movies, a Grace Kelly line of apparel, and an Audrey Hepburn cosmetics line. We did deals for Mariah Carey, and Kiefer Sutherland, and represented Celine Dion, Gloria Estefan, Michael Jackson, and a myriad of other artists as the agent for Sony Music.

As great as all of this was, in 2008 during a trip to Dubai, where we had established a joint venture with Rubicon, a Jordanian media company, I received a call from a U.S. client saying that they couldn't find $1 million in payments due from us. Huh? Did I know where it was? What? *No, Sunamori and his team handle all the financials, but I'm sure it's just a mistake.*

I was in the back of my friend Ghassan's BMW somewhere near the Burj Khalifa (the soon-to-be tallest building in the world), which was then under construction, and I called Sunamori in Tokyo.

"Hey," I said, "our client just called saying that they are missing a million bucks. Do you know anything about that?"

He was quiet for a beat. Then he said, "I've been using it to pay my employee salaries."

I didn't get it. I said, "Ok, so when are you going to pay our client?"

Another beat. "I can't."

At that moment it hit me: He was stealing. Although I wasn't privy to his books, it had always seemed like he lived bigger than the revenue he had coming in. Nothing blatant, but he had a boat, a nice car, and a nice apartment in the center of Tokyo. He also had 15 employees for his business, which, by the recession of 2008, didn't make sense. He had apparently started keeping the money he owed to the studios to support it all.

It turned out that through various accounting loopholes he had withheld millions of dollars from both Japanese and American clients. For the next two years, I spent my time trying to fix it by negotiating payment terms, which he ultimately couldn't uphold. I loved Sunamori. We had spent 15 years doing some really great deals together. But when he withheld $60,000 from me, I quit.

We didn't speak for nearly two years. But on a hot, muggy morning in July 2012, I sat down with him in a quaint coffee shop in the middle of Tokyo to catch up. He had reached out to me several weeks earlier saying that, after two years, he thought it would be great to get together. I said sure—life's too short to hold grudges on anyone (as you'll see later, even priests). I realized long before that he had much bigger problems than I did—he closed his company and filed for bankruptcy several months after I left—and in my heart, I had gotten over the money soon after our breakup. It's always a two-way street; could I have worked harder during the time I was with him? Anyway, since I was going to be in Tokyo in a few weeks . . . why not.

It was really good to see him. He said he was sorry, that the business had just gotten out of hand and he couldn't stop using other people's money. Talk about an opportunity to apply the Get To Principle. I had great appreciation for my life, and incredible compassion for his. I smiled. We didn't talk about the money he had taken from me. We both, in a Japanese kind of way, agreed that the past was the past.

Sunamori told me he was representing a J-Pop music group called Bijomen Z. Their webpage says this: "The world's first all-male girls band consisting of four men who are more beautiful than women." Basically, they were four cross-dressing Japanese guys, led by a flamboyant nut (I say this with affection) named Yakkun, singing punk rock. They were going to be performing a concert in Paris the coming September, and Sunamori asked if I would come and translate (Japanese to English, anyway) for him and the band as they did a week of touring around the city. They would pay my expenses. Let bygones be bygones, as they say. I went, and our time in Paris was wild, with concerts, after-parties, and a parade of hundreds of cross dressers and other too-wild-for-words human beings that went from the Arc du Triomphe down the Champs Elysees to the Louvre. It was nice to be reconnected with Sunamori, who had an incredible flair for life. Together we had ridden camels in the deserts of Dubai, presented the Bon Jovi kids' animation show concept to Jon in a swanky hotel board-room in London, spent time with each other's families, and had too-many-to-name experiences that come with negotiating many millions of dollars in deals over 15 years. There in Paris, we committed to rebuild our once-flourishing friendship.

●●●●

However, two weeks after returning from Paris, that rebuilding abruptly came to an end. I received a call from a friend in Osaka. "Ted," they said somberly, "Sunamori and Yakkun have died in a car accident."

What the fuck? I thought. "What happened?" I asked. Apparently, Sunamori and the band were driving from Tokyo to Hiroshima in the south to do a concert. Their minivan crashed into the center divider of a deserted highway. It was dark and rainy, and when Sunamori got out of the van to flag for help, a car came by and hit him. He died instantly. Yakkun got out of the car to help Sunamori, and he was hit by the next car coming by. He died in the hospital later that night. What the hell?

I flew over a few days later for the funeral, held at a nonde-script funeral home on the outskirts of Tokyo. After arriving, on October 7, 2013, I posted the following on Facebook:

"As I was looking out the window during the one-hour train ride from the Tokyo airport into the city, in the distance was a pagoda silhouetted by the setting sun, with the closer country-side of bamboo and rice fields racing by. The sound of the train tracks. It was a stunning, awe-inspiring moment. And I realized: I was having the privilege, the grace, the honor of being able to experience and feel that moment. As a human, I get to do that. Even now, in this hotel room I get to experience the tears of missing my friend. How lucky am I? Sunamori reminded me of living in this moment often by living so fully and passionately in everything he did. He's continuing to do it now. By realizing that he doesn't get to experience THIS anymore, I can hear him saying: 'Ted, this is it! Get over whatever has happened and live now in this moment! This . . . is . . . it!' I don't know about you guys, but I'm ready to live! Thanks, yet again, Sunamori!"

At the funeral home on that cool October night, along with several hundred other people, I waited in a line that snaked out the door into the parking lot. Everyone was wearing a black funeral suit or dress, the standard attire for these occasions in Japan. I had a dark blue suit on—it was the best I had. There was a lot of bowing (I had learned years earlier with Mitsuko that the Japanese don't hug) as past friends and associates of Sunamori's had one last chance to cross paths. I saw many people I hadn't seen for years and it was good to reconnect. The Japanese are a pretty stoic bunch so there was not a lot of crying, although you could hear plenty of sniffles amongst the hushed conversations.

After an hour or so I entered the room, set up like a church, rows of folding chairs on either side with an aisle leading down the center to the casket, opened, on a table at the front of the room. It was surrounded by hundreds of flower arrangements, each with a sign with the name of who had sent it—I noticed "Sunworld" on one. In the rows of chairs, sitting in silence (and all in black) were the family of Sunamori on one side and his wife, Kiyo, on the other. As I slowly made my way to the front, I noticed Kiyo and their nine-year-old daughter, Rika, sitting to the left of the casket, alone. As each person got to the front, they would light an incense stick and put it in a sand-filled bowl, clap their hands prayer style in front of them, bow to Sunamori, turn and bow to the family behind them, and last of all, face back to Kiyo and bow to her. Staring straight ahead with a blank stare, she would bow her head back. No tears. She was in a trance, not really seeing, going through the ritualistic motions of the culturally steeped Japanese funeral process.

It was my turn. I stepped up to the coffin and bowed to Sunamori's lifeless body, trying to hold back the tears. I turned and bowed to the family, and they all bowed their heads back to me. But when I turned back to face Kiyo, instead of bowing, I just looked at her, tears welling up in my eyes. When she looked up and saw it was me, we both lost it. We had become close friends over the last 18 years but had not been in contact since I had quit working with Sunamori several years prior. Breaking all tradition, she jumped up and ran into my arms and we stood there sobbing together. I couldn't hear, but could feel the gasps from the room as this foreigner stood hugging (God forbid) the now-widowed Kiyo. But I didn't care. Stoicism is not in my dictionary. She was getting to grieve openly, if only briefly. After several minutes, we settled down, and after hugging Rika, I told Kiyo I would be around for the next morning's second service. She returned to her seat for what was to be at least another hour of painful head-bowing. It was silent as I walked away.

As promised, I arrived back at the funeral home the next morning, where a more intimate crowd of about 50 people gathered for a blessing by a bald, black-robed Buddhist monk. I found Kiyo and we hugged and said, basically, "What the hell happened? What is this life all about?" and cried. She called him an asshole for dying and laughed. I laughed because I knew there was no right or wrong way to handle death. She said she missed him terribly—they had been together for 25 years, and only 10 years ago conceived little Rika. The ceremony was sweet, with incense burning and a low chanting by the monk, and each one of us threw a flower on his body as we, again, passed by his coffin.

After it was over, we all went outside and stood lining the driveway as black-suited, white-gloved attendants carried the casket out to a waiting hearse, and the family and the monk boarded a 20-seat mini-bus that would take them to the crematorium for a final private farewell.

The hearse loaded, the family on board the bus, there was a pause. The small bus doors reopened and the white-gloved driver came out and started walking down the line of us on the driveway. As he got closer I realized he was saying, "Larkins San. Larkins San. Is Larkins San here?" I stepped out of the line, and he looked at me and said, "Would you like to board the bus?" (although it wasn't stated as a question). I know this isn't appropriate but I thought, *Hell yeah!* As I boarded I caught Kiyo's eye and she, if only slightly, nodded. I took the one empty seat next to Sunamori's brother on the silent ride to what was to be yet another life-changing, Get To experience.

When we arrived, our small group followed a white-gloved (there is a lot of white-glove wearing in Japan) attendant pushing the coffin, which was on a stainless-steel table with wheels, to a small wood-paneled room. Once inside, the top was opened and again, we lit incense and bowed and this time, more intimately, said our goodbyes. This time we all cried as the monk slowly chanted. After 20 minutes or so, the attendant, an expressionless woman of about 30 years, asked if we were complete. When we all nodded she slowly closed the top and pushed the casket, all of us silently following, out a back door and into a long, darkened hallway. As we walked, we passed several places with short, four-foot-tall, elevator-like doors where similar wheeled tables, minus the caskets, were parked. There must have been 20 sets of doors running the length of the hall. Through tiny windows in the thick metal doors you could see fire inside.

We came to a vacant spot and the attendant parked the foot of the casket in front of the doors. We gathered around. After more chants by the monk, the attendant slowly, deliberately pulled opened the doors of the yet-to-be-lit oven. We all put our hands on the coffin and started pushing it slowly off the table onto a metal rack inside—at first whispering through our tears, "Goodbye Sunamori," crescendoing into an all-out wailing of, "I love you!"—"Thank you for everything!"—"Rest in peace son!"—and the toughest to hear, over and over through her sobs, "Bye daddy, I miss you!"

The coffin slid in place and the attendant closed the doors. We stood sniffling but otherwise quiet and I felt a finality I had never felt before in my life. It was a finality that would be overshadowed a short time later. The attendant said, "Please follow me," and we slowly followed her to a room upstairs.

Awaiting us was a feast of sushi, tempura, and a myriad of other traditional Japanese dishes. The 20 of us sat on tatami mats on the floor at low tables, and over several beers and drinks of sake, there was a lot of conversation, some laughing and fun storytelling. I sat next to Sunamori's father, Hajime. I had not met him before, and he was quite interested in the experiences I had shared with his son. It was sweet. I could tell he was a gracious and caring man. But he was stoic, holding back tears and, his Japanese background aside, I had an idea why. Over the years, Sunamori had shared much with me about his life, and one thing in particular was about his dad. In 1945, an 18-year-old Hajime was a kamikaze pilot. *How can that be?* you ask. Apparently, he had taken off on his mission to crash into a U.S. ship off the coast of Japan but had engine troubles and crash-landed on a small island. He was rescued, returned to base, and given another mission. But before he could take off, there was another malfunction, and his mission was again postponed. Then the bombs at Hiroshima and Nagasaki were dropped, and that was that. He went on to own a business, get married, and have a family, including my friend Sunamori.

I got to sit there with Hajime and his other children and talk about our respective lives. It wasn't appropriate to ask about his kamikaze experience at that moment, but I couldn't help wondering how much indoctrination it took to get this man, when he was young, to take off in that plane. I don't believe there was much Get To in it. As I've said, over the years I had learned about the brutality and atrocities of the Japanese during the war. I'd visited the Pacific island of Saipan, where 30,000 Japanese soldiers and 20,000 Japanese civilians died fighting to the death and, on that same island, I stood on "Suicide Cliff," where over 1,000 Japanese men, women, and children jumped to their deaths rather than be taken prisoner when the U.S. troops came ashore. Nearly 4,000 U.S. soldiers died. So I understood the resentment and negative sentiment my dad and others of an older generation could have toward the Japanese. But I do think that if he were sitting there with Hajime as he grieved his son's death, Dad might have had a Get To moment and said to Hajime, "I'm so sorry for your loss." He might even have hugged him. The Japanese were brutal in World War II, but even an indoctrinated teenager can change, as Hajime did, to being someone who raised such a beautiful being as Sunamori.

After two or so hours, conversations were settling down when the attendant, white gloves on, came in and asked us to follow her. We silently walked back downstairs and arrived in yet another room, this one much smaller. A few minutes after standing there, a door in the back of the room opened and another young woman wheeled in a much smaller stainless-steel cart on which was a cookie-jar-sized urn, and next to it a pile of ashes and bones that was once Sunamori. I was stunned. It was surreal. Even now, years later, I shiver at the image of that cart being wheeled into that dimly lit room. Another image I have is of being handed a chopstick, and with another person, using the chopstick we each held, picking up the larger bone parts and together dropping them into the urn. After we all had a turn, the attendant, using her own pair of chopsticks, expertly picked up bones and said, "This was his knee cap." "This was his cheekbone." "This was part of his skull." One at a time she respectfully dropped them in, beginning with his feet and working her way up to his head (so he wasn't upside down). Like I said, surreal.

When the urn started to overflow, she used her white-gloved fist to pack more in. Crunch, crunch, crunch. She then used a mini–dust pan and paintbrush-sized broom to delicately sweep up every last spec of ash. Finally she screwed a lid on, wrapped it in a beautiful piece of cloth and handed it to Kiyo. That, my friends, is finality. Rika holding a large photo of Sunamori, and Kiyo in the lead holding the urn, we slowly walked back to the bus and silently returned to the mortuary to say goodbye.

A few weeks later I flew back and spent a day and a night with Kiyo and Rika. I got to experience being with their heartache. For dinner and breakfast, they set a place for Sunamori, putting food and hot tea out for him. The shrine they built in the house with his urn and various photos was piled high with flowers and mementos. We talked, and laughed, and cried. Rikka and I, in their small apartment, danced. It was so sweet. Because we had put flowers on his body, pushed his casket into the furnace, and put his bones in the urn, there was no denial that Sunamori was dead. We were complete, and they began the process of moving on with life. I reflect on that experience often, remembering the pain of their loss and yet their ability to accept what is.

But here's the thing: Three years after that, in June 2015, I was having coffee with a couple of Japanese folks I had been introduced to who were in L.A. They'd had some business dealings with Sunamori in the past and we were chatting about him. As great a guy as Sunamori was, no matter how many friends he had, he had become extremely reckless financially, and his use of other people's money had gotten way out of control. Apparently, I only knew a small part of the story.

One of the guys said, "When Sunamori was murdered, how did you feel?"

At that moment this notion, this feeling that had festered in me for years, this unknowable knowing that the accident wasn't an accident, rose to the surface. The Japanese mafia—the *yakuza*—had gotten him. He had taken too much money to let go. And Yakkun was a victim of the play of Sunamori's life. Now, just to be clear, I don't know and I'm not accusing anyone. The only thing I know about the *yakuza* is what I learned in the 1989 film *Black Rain*, with Michael Douglas, which I saw being filmed in Osaka when I first arrived. That means I really don't know anything. I said to the Japanese guy, *"Uso tsuki"* (that means "liar" in Japanese). I told him I still believed it was an accident. He said something like, "Whatever," and left me with it.

Recently I asked Yoshida what he thought and he said simply, "Accident, accident," and changed the subject.

I get to still wonder.

Practice

We've all grieved, and at some point we've all been asked, by life, to let go. My kids did it recently with their pet hamster; they loved that little creature. It's not easy. Letting go of lost money, a lost job, or a lost relationship requires being present and accepting the pain that comes with that. And truly being with that pain, acknowledging it, is the first step, maybe one of many of steps, toward letting go. Whether it be days or years or even a lifetime, letting go can have a profound effect on your life.

Get To—Smile—Goodbye, friend.

Sunamori and me, Dubai, 2008.

Studio execs celebrating Sunamori,
Los Angeles, October 2013.

Yakkun (far right) and the Bijoman group,
Paris, 2013.

Sunamori and Rika, 2003.

29. Get To Life Partner

The concept of monogamy is overrated, until you find someone you want to hang out with the rest of your life.

Of all the goings-on in life, one special event happened on Friday, March 18, 1994: I got to meet Beth. Blah, blah, blah on how couples meet, so I'll keep this short. Beth has an entirely different version—but I'm sticking with mine.

Dale, a young guy I had recently met who was working in real-estate development in Osaka, wanted to go out for drinks on that Friday night and suggested we meet at the English-language school where he used to teach. The school had a party on Friday nights for the Japanese students to mingle casually with the foreign teachers. Free beer and snacks, not a bad way to start the night, so I agreed.

I showed up, grabbed a drink, and was standing chatting with some Japanese kid when across the room I saw a very cute *gaijin* girl. I said "See ya" to the Japanese guy and walked over.

"Hi, my name's Ted, what's yours?"

"My name's Beth," she said. "Want some pretzels?" She offered me some.

I said, "What are you doing here in Japan?"

"I came here on an exchange program from Emory University. I met a Japanese guy and fell in love and decided to stay. I've been here eight years and I'm either going to marry the guy or go back home."

Oh. "Where's home?"

"Dad's in Connecticut, Mom's in St. Croix—Virgin Islands. I grew up in both places as a kid."

Oh really? The Virgin Islands sounded nice. I liked her already.

By this time, our eyes were locked and I said, as a joke, "I think we met in a past life."

She smiled. She told me she was going to be taking a "spiritual awakening" seminar in Sydney in May and asked if I wanted to come. *Hell, yeah!* I was all about spiritual awakening, and besides, she could have asked me to go to an accounting seminar in Des Moines and I would have said, "Hell, yeah."

Dale showed up, and a group of us went out to some bars. I don't remember much, except that Beth and I talked and talked and talked. Six weeks later we met in the Blue Mountains of Australia and did a week-long course called Avatar, a beautiful teaching about the exploration of consciousness. We skydived, scuba-dived the Great Barrier Reef, and rode a motorcycle through the rain forests—and fell in love. We returned home and she moved in with me and the Yoshidas. Twenty-two years and three kids later, Beth still teaches Avatar, and we still talk and talk and talk. *Get To—Smile—Fall in love.*

Practice

Think about your significant other. If you don't have one, think about yourself. Remember a particularly fun time together (or alone). On a Caribbean-warm evening, low clouds threatening rain, standing on a beach in St. Croix, committing to spend the rest of my life with Beth. Wow. Recognize that even though there may have been challenges, the overall love is what matters. Even if you've gotten divorced, appreciate the intention that was there. Love yourself.

Get To—Smile—Love.

30. Get To Go Home

"Where we love is home—
home that our feet may leave,
but not our hearts."
—*Oliver Wendell Holmes, Sr.*

On June 12, 1995, a year after we met, Beth and I were married in Osaka. Beth's visa to stay in Japan had run out, but, by being my wife, she could continue to stay. Don't get me wrong, we were in love and planned to get married at some point anyway. But this was an easy fix for that always-daunting visa dilemma.

We walked ten minutes down to the small local city office and filled out some paperwork. A dismal, unenthused city clerk in a gray uniform stamped the papers with a seal and handed a copy back to us. Unlike many Japanese in Osaka in the '90s, he wasn't impressed that we spoke the language. It didn't matter; we were married . . . I think. I say that because we just filled out some papers and handed them to a guy in a rundown city office on the outskirts of Osaka. In the 19 years that we've been back in the States, no one has asked to see if we're married. Not the IRS, not the banks, not the car-loan people. We just say we're married, and that's enough. Thank God, because whatever "marriage certificate" he handed us was lost a long time ago.

Our respective parents dissatisfied with an Osaka elopement, we decided to have a ceremony acknowledging our union on a beach in St. Croix. I didn't fall in love with Beth because of her comment about her mom living there, but it sure has come in handy. It was the first of dozens of trips we've made over the years to that beautiful island. We had given plenty of notice to extended family and friends about the event, and on June 14, 1996, seventy people gathered there and celebrated us. But as the ten days' festivities of scuba diving, plantation tours, long relaxed hours on the various beaches, and incredible meals were winding down, and everyone was anticipating their trips home, Beth and I realized we weren't anticipating ours. Beth asked, "Do you want to move back to the U.S.?"

"Hell, yeah!" I said.

We had spent an amazing two years together in Osaka. Beth began taking Japanese lessons with Sensei and the three of us often went hiking, or just hung out with her at her house drinking tea. Beth and I spent a lot of time in the ancient cities of Kyoto and Nara visiting the many shrines and temples. Our big night out was Friday, when we got on our bikes, grabbed a bottle of wine, and headed to our friend Liz's house to watch the show *Friends*. It was a big deal in 1995 and Liz had—get this—*satellite TV*. A big deal indeed! A group of us, mostly *gaijin*, would gather to drink and eat cheese and crackers for an hour before the show came on. Then we would watch the unfolding of the lives of Ross, Rachel, and the gang, as each of us in our own minds remembered how life had been, and probably at some point would be again, outside Japan.

Of our many experiences, one in particular stands out: On January 17, 1995, at 5:46 a.m., a sweet dream about Beth turned into a nightmare as our building started shaking violently. Falling out of bed, we ran from doorway to doorway wondering which one might protect us after the building collapsed. Afterwards I felt a little silly because, really, if the building came down, no bathroom doorway was going to save us.

Anyway, a lifetime of seconds (20 to be exact) passed and when the shaking subsided, the building was cracked but intact. The hanging lamp in my room still swaying, I stepped over books and picture frames strewn on the floor and turned on the TV to see a scrolling news feed: "Kobe suffers major earthquake, at least 7 people dead." Kobe was only 18 miles from our building in Osaka, but far enough that we didn't get the brunt of it. Within the hour, the news feed at the top of the screen—now rolling above early morning images of buildings toppled, people panicking, and cars crushed under collapsed bridges—read, "Kobe suffers major earthquake, at least 50 people dead." Shit, this was bad.

The day before, executives from Lucasfilm had arrived in town; we were going to be pitching to be the agent for the *Star Wars* merchandise program that morning. We had a plan to sell a boatload of *Star Wars* stuff to the Japanese. However, when they arrived at our offices at 11 the morning of the earthquake, the execs were too scared from the ensuing aftershocks to pay attention to our presentation. One jet-lagged lady had been up and in the hotel bath when the earth began to shake, and, according to her, she almost drowned. All they could think about was getting out of town and up to Tokyo. We never had a chance at that business.

In truth, I didn't really care about business or a couple of traumatized Americans. My Japan had suffered a terrible event— that evening the news was reporting up to 1,000 dead. The next day, I awoke to the news of mounting deaths, now at 2,500, and decided to go help. A few days later, with all transportation to Kobe still cut off, I hitched a ride into the devastation on the back of a rickety motorcycle with a young *Time Magazine* reporter from New York named Tom. I couldn't believe what I saw: The city, with a population of 1.3 million, was wrecked. Large, blackened areas where fires had raged, some still burning, houses now piles of rubble, entire elevated highways on their sides. We weaved around long, deep cracks in the pavement and came to one of the toppled buildings; once probably eight stories, it was now lying across the road, like it had been built on its side. It had simply fallen over. We detoured and kept going and came to a large, severely damaged three-story building with hundreds of people out front. We stopped and spent the cold, clear day helping any way we could, mostly distributing water and blankets to the dazed residents. When someone told me the building had once been five stories, and that the middle two stories simply pancaked, I stared in disbelief. The death toll of the Kobe earthquake eventually reached more than 6,400. It was worse than bad.

Yoshida, completely unnerved, asked us to move out so he could tear down the building. He did just that and put a solid concrete structure in its place. Beth and I rented an apartment on our own. My six-year homestay had come to an end.

Upon our return to Osaka from St Croix, I asked Yoshida if I could move back to the States and open an office there. But, no, that wasn't going to happen. Yoshida liked how it was in Japan with me there. So I took a different tack: "Yoshida," I said, "You've been an incredible mentor. I've lived with your family for six years and learned Japanese, learned business, and I'm grateful beyond measure for all you've done for me. But I'm done in Japan. I'm moving back to the U.S. I'd be happy to open an office for you there."

Almost a year later, on March 1, 1997, with our possessions on a boat and pet cat Pearl in hand, Beth and I flew to Los Angeles to start a new life setting up Sunworld, USA.

Practice

Remember your wedding ceremony, if you had one, or a memorable birthday party. Really sink down and remember the details: was it a big event? Very private? Was it held in a church? If so, recall everything you can: what the empty church smelled like in the quiet before the ceremony, with all the flowers around (if you happened to be there for that). Or what the office sounded like as you waited in the hall for the justice of the peace. Were there hugs? Think of how it felt to hug an elderly relative, the smooth or prickly cheek, the scent of aftershave. Most of all, remember the person you married, their expression as the final moment arrived, the feel of their hands in yours— or if it's a different memorable event, remember those you loved best on that day.

Get To—Smile—Celebrate!

Our good friend Phillip marrying Beth and me on the
beach in St. Croix, U.S. Virgin Islands, June 1996.

31. Get To Cancer

"The warrior is the one who shows up, ready for anything, expecting nothing, and from this, his most inner known self directs what stands in need of his presence and goodness. He can then expand into the direction of goodness ready to emerge."

—*J.D. Davidson, mentor and executive coach*

We met up with Nick often over the years, either at the places he called home (Dallas, Honolulu, Portland) or when he visited our place in Southern California. One day in 2001 I got a call.

"Brother Ted," he said, "I got the cancer." *What?* I asked him how bad. "Well, melanoma, so not pretty, but I'll fight it."

And he did fight. For a year and half, through all the chemo and other drugs. He was a doctor and was very hands-on with his treatment, and knew the right specialists to see. At one point it seemed to have gone away. Beth and I were hiking with him in the hills outside Portland in April 2002, and as a celebration I said I would buy all of us (with my bazillions of airline miles) tickets to Italy, one country Nick and I had wanted to visit. Beth had been there and would be our tour guide. I bought the tickets for an October trip.

Nick and I also agreed to do Vipassana, a ten-day silent meditation retreat, that July. Beth would not be part of that craziness—just Nicky and me. But a week before the retreat, to be held at a ranch in the Sierra Nevada Mountains, Nick called and said, "Brother Ted, the cancer is back. It's bad. I can't go meditate." Shit. Nicky!

So I went to meditate by myself. There's not much to say about ten days of silent meditation. Really, it's just ten days of sitting in silence. There were several hundred crazies like me there. *Who are these nuts?* I thought. After registration and an information meeting, I silently walked the dirt path through the trees to my cabin, with bunk beds for 16 people. You didn't even acknowledge the other guys. Not a nod or smile. Silence, both physically and mentally. I set up my space in a bottom bunk, and that would be my home for the next ten days. Every morning we woke up to a gong at 4 a.m., sat for several hours, and walked silently to breakfast, where "staff" served us in silence. We'd go back to the cabin and take a nap, go meditate, go to lunch, take a nap, meditate, go to diner, meditate, go to sleep. Simple, right? NOT.

My mind was like a freight train. *What the fuck am I doing here over the Fourth of July? Am I crazy? Nick is sick, I should be with him! And I'm horny for my babe. And my legs are killing me and I can barely sit without pain. At least at a Zen temple you can talk! And my bunk mates are serial killers doing some kind of mandatory rehab! I could wake up wrapped in duct tape with a sock in my mouth!* Honestly, I thought I was going out of my mind. Yet I kept sitting. Finally, on day 7, it got quiet. Not all of a sudden like in Japan, but at lunch, sitting out on a bench overlooking the mountains, I got to feel a stillness that was beyond calm. I smiled. In the meditations that followed, although there was pain in my legs, I looked at it simply as a sensation—and smiled more. By day 10, I was full of such joy for life I cried while sitting on my cushion.

At the end, when we could talk, packing our things in what had been our home, I found that my bunk mates were the most incredible humans, each on their own life journey. I'll say it again: Who am I to judge anyone, ever?

As I got in the car and turned on my phone there were a couple of messages. One was from Nick: "Brother Ted, you need to come to Portland."

Practice

This sounds simple, but it may be the most difficult practice—and the most rewarding. When you first wake up, the moment you come to consciousness, even before your eyes open, do the following: Whisper "Get To." Smile. Then say, "Be alive." "Get To." Smile. "Be alive." I have found that the smiling part is what's challenging. I say, "Get To," but eking out the smile, as my brain kicks into gear, can be tough. But I do it, and after just a few minutes, I can't wait to get out of bed and start the day. Do it every single day.

Get To—Smile—Be alive.

32. Get To Live and Die with Nick

Today I was feeling a little pouty. But I decided to smile. In honor of Nick. I owe it to him. I always have said that what I'm missing in life is the death experience. Now I have a full-on one. Even with his passing, it's still my choice to be happy.
—Journal entry, Costa Mesa, July 25, 2002,
one week after Nick died

Nick's cancer had returned with a vengeance. He figured he had only three to six months to live, and he was going to have a party. So Beth and I jumped on a plane and went to Portland. There were 100-plus people at his house, in his yard, everywhere. Many had shaved their heads in his honor. Doctors, nurses, people from all over. His brother and parents were there. At one point, a bunch of us were in the living room and the Cat Stevens' song "Miles from Nowhere" came on. Nick sang out in his raspy, dying voice:

Lord my body has been a good friend

But I won't need it when I reach the end

Miles from nowhere

I guess I'll take my time

Oh yeah, to reach there

We all bawled our eyes out.

Through the course of the evening, people slowly said their goodbyes, and Beth and I went to our hotel, saying we'd see him in the morning. We got to be at an end-of-life party.

The next morning we showed up at 9 a.m. and there were just two or three friends hanging around. After a few minutes, Nick asked me to see him in the basement.

I said, "What's up, brother Nick?"

"Ted, ever since that first week at the Zen temple, I knew you were a special soul," he said, "especially when you said, 'I feel like I can eat the air!'"

"Thanks Nick, that's why we call each other Brother."

He ignored that and said, "So I need some time with you and need you to have Beth leave."

Really? This was an odd development, but I said, "Sure, Nick." I didn't understand but went upstairs and told Beth. She hated it, but, crying, gave Nick a huge hug goodbye, saying she'd see him soon. I drove her to the airport.

When I returned to the house 45 minutes later, Nick, his mom and dad, my good-friend-to-be Josiah, and an ex-girlfriend of Nick's were sitting in the living room. Although I had only just met them the day before, I could feel they were sweet people. I smiled at everyone, and, looking around, noticed that a hospital bed had been set up in the middle of the main room. It was surrounded by flowers and had a few chairs on either side. I looked at Nick and asked, "What's going on?"

"Brother Ted, my cancer is bad and getting worse. I have a few months at best. And it will be horrendous and painful. I'm a doctor and I've seen the suffering too many times. I'm ready to go now, on my terms. And I need you to help."

I didn't understand what that meant. But I soaked in the surroundings, the new people, the aroma of the sandalwood incense (maybe he'd gotten it in Japan), the quiet mood, and at last I smiled.

Nick went to the bathroom and asked me to follow. Both of us standing in front of the mirror, I said, "Hey man, what's up? What do you mean you need my help?"

He coughed, took in a wheezy breath, looked slowly at me, then pulled out a pocket knife and opened the blade. As he slowly brought it to his throat I grabbed his wrist and said, "Nicky, what the fuck?"

"Just kiddin', Brother Ted," he said, and laughed as he put the knife on the counter. My heart pounded.

Then he told me, standing there in the bathroom, that he had planned a ritual where the five of us would help him OD on morphine.

I said, "Nick, I love you, but I can't do this."

He said, "Brother Ted, of all the people in the world, I know you can help." Holding on to the counter top to balance, he walked slowly out of the room. I stood there in a trance. I could leave. There was a rental car outside. This was a moment of calling in life. What do you do? *You get to make choices*—I stayed.

We spent the next several hours talking, helping Nick walk in the garden, smelling the flowers. Literally! Then at about 3 p.m. he said, "It's time." He slowly went inside and lay on the bed in the living room. We gathered around. His mom said, "We're going to use this dropper and take turns filling it with morphine from this bottle, then put it into Nick's mouth. It should take about 30 minutes, and Nick will slowly lose consciousness and die. After he dies, per his request, we'll follow Tibetan ritual, so we won't touch his body for one hour."

My heart was pounding. *Really?* I couldn't help thinking, *Could I go to jail for this?* But the big question was, what did I feel in my heart? I got quiet in that moment and looked at Nick. Our eyes met. I felt that my dearest friend was suffering, and was asking for help. He had tried for years to fight the cancer—and lost. We all knew it. He had called hospice and was under their care. Nick was hacking and had difficulty breathing and it was getting worse daily. I thought, *I get to do this for my friend.* I couldn't know what Nick was thinking. He was, quite literally, on the verge of death. But there was a glint in his eye that told me he was at peace. We held each other's gaze and grinned as tears filled our eyes. It was time.

I was closest to Nick's head so was first to go. I took the dropper and said, "Are you sure?"

He smiled and said, "Sometimes you gotta quit holding on. I'm ready."

I squeezed the liquid into his mouth, and handed the bottle to Josiah. We took turns, slowly, crying with him at times, laughing with him at others, as we loved this man and his journey in the life/death cycle. He asked that Josiah and I become friends. (We're best friends to this day.) Nick had a peaceful look on his face the whole time. At one point, it felt as though he was holding on, and I said, "Brother, relax. Let go. It's okay to let go."

Slowly he fell asleep. His breaths grew shorter and shorter, and finally stopped. We sat there for a long time, the rare Portland sun shining through the partly drawn blinds. Each of us in our own world, created by our own thoughts, was experiencing that moment. I sat quietly appreciating my friend's lifeless body, but feeling he was still there. We slowly got up and went for a walk in the nearby mountains. As I took each step it felt amazing to be alive, knowing that we would all be dead at some point. I stopped, listening to the birds, the buzz of insects, the footsteps of the other humans walking ahead of me. I looked up at the blue sky through the tall trees and I thought, *That we get to do this thing called life, for the briefest moments of time, is a miracle beyond any definition we might give to the word.*

●●●●

I was about eight years old, walking through a graveyard near my grandmother's house, when I came across an old gravestone and read it. The words have been with me to this day:

Look and see as you walk by

As you are now so once was I

As I am now so you must be

Prepare for death and follow me

For a long time I thought it was quite a morbid quote from a morbid person. But lately I've come to think of the author as a gentle soul, offering sweet advice: Don't take it all so seriously.

I think my gravestone will be this:

You Get To have experiences

Dead people, like me, don't

Enjoy your life every moment

I guess that's more like a Haiku, remnants from my days in Japan, but it's the best I can do.

Like Nick, we're all going to die. We get to live. We get to die. Period. My grandparents are dead, my mom and dad are dead, many of my friends are dead. I don't dwell on it, but every once in a while I wonder, *How am I going to die?* Of course, I have the fantasy of dying on the 18th green at St Andrews Links, making a 30-foot putt for birdie at 102 years of age. The putt goes in, I raise my arms in a V-for-victory pose, and my heart seizes up. I smile and look up and say, "Thank You," in a whisper. I smile, fall to my knees, then slowly fall over and die. No one hurries around or is panicked trying to save me. In fact, maybe they all clap.

Anyway, it could be cancer in five years. Or a car accident tomorrow. Or heck, a gunshot wound on the way to work in L.A. (I saw a guy today on the subway who scared the shit out of me.) The point is to bring the Get To Principle to dying. Can I smile, at the moment of truth, and say: "I Get To do this right here and now"?

Here's a story:

In 1990, I was on a plane from Seoul to Hong Kong. It was a huge, lumbering 747 and I was in the back in a middle seat. It was dark and stormy outside. Inside, it was crowded and stinky; smoking on planes still existed and the Koreans are known for their garlic consumption. The guys on either side of me smelled like garlic, raw onions, and stale beer combined. Finally, after five hours I could feel the descent, the sound of the landing gear engaging, the normal rattles and moans of that massive piece of metal hurtling through the air.

All of a sudden there was a loud, jolting sound, like the engines were being torn off, and the plane started shaking violently. The air masks dropped, people started screaming as handbags and other items flew through the cabin. We were going to crash—my heart pounded—and I grinned. Not quite a smile, but I grinned. *Wow*, I said to myself, *this is what it's like.* I started laughing. I know that sounds glib, and either I was in denial or I'm a lunatic, but in that moment I laughed. Do you remember in *Planes, Trains and Automobiles*, where John Candy and Steve Martin are driving the wrong way on a freeway and pass between two oncoming semis? And John turns into the Devil, laughing? That was me (except without the evil part).

Instead of hitting the ground as anticipated, we could feel the plane start to ascend, still shaking, people crying, the sound of the engines deafening. The plane continued to gain altitude, then smoothed out, and ten minutes later we were back on approach. We landed and taxied to the gate. No announcement was made, not even "Welcome to Hong Kong." Sniffling and shaking or simply dazed, people gathered their things and deplaned. I still grinned. (I speculate that coming down through the low clouds, the pilot at the last second saw something on the runway and aborted landing. Full throttle of those massive engines at that moment caused the intense shaking and sensation of crashing. I'll never know.)

To be fair, if I were getting tortured, I'm pretty sure I couldn't have that viewpoint on death. Back in the 1970s, there was a show called *Kung Fu*, starring David Carradine as Caine, a wandering monk. He was called Grasshopper by his mentor, Master Po, and looking back, I believe this show was my first awakening to spirituality. One episode in particular affected me and how I looked at life then, and how I live it now. Caine and two other guys are put in separate wood boxes, just barely big enough for them to fit, out in a barren field in the desert heat. For three days. It was punishment for something they allegedly did, but of course, Caine didn't do. Anyway, after three brutally hot days the guards open the boxes, one at a time, and the first two guys come spilling out, on the edge of death. They open the third box and nothing happens. The camera pans over and looks inside, and there sits Caine, cross-legged and with a peaceful smile. He steps out, blinks a few times, takes a sip of an offered cup of water and walks off. I have always fantasized that I could do that. I mean, if Caine could be so at peace like that, couldn't I? I hope I never have to find out.

So I think about dying a little. I contemplate the reality of dying. That's pretty cool. Sometimes I think, *If I died right now, what would everyone think? They would be so sad, right? They would say, "He was such a nice guy."* Probably, but in reality, after some grieving, be it days or weeks, that would be it, and I'd be a memory like my dad, or Michael Jackson. "How am I going to die?" is a great thought, but I don't dwell on it too much. I get to live now, in the present, so keeping my attention on the evolving moment is for me the most effective way to live a satisfying life. I know that's the way Nick lived.

Practice

Years before his death, Nick, Beth, and I were walking leisurely in the Back Bay, an inland delta nature reserve in Newport Beach, California. There are miles of dirt trails that weave through the marshland, all kinds of desert vegetation and some wildlife flitting around. It was a cool early morning, dew still on the ground. At one point Nick stopped and took a handful of leaves from a plant and smushed them up. He held a fistful to my face. "Sage, Brother Ted, smell that." I took a huge breath in through my nose and was overwhelmed at the scent. We truly stopped to smell the roses.

Imagine you have three months to live. Think about how you would spend them, maybe smelling the flowers. Think of how intense each sensation would be if you knew it was one of your last: the weight of a toddler on your lap, the feel of your dog's head on your knee, the scent of Scotch tape, the sound of your significant other's breathing while asleep.

Get To—Smile—Appreciate life.

Nick (with me and Beth) just before he died, April 2003.

33. Get To Be Pregnant

May I encounter the perfect
obstacles in my path.
—Tibetan prayer

After Nick died that July day in 2002, I flew back home and told Beth the story, and we sobbed together and had amazing, life-affirming lovemaking. A few weeks later, on August 10—my 40th birthday—she did a pregnancy test, and it was positive. It was like it was part of Nick's plan. Beth and I had talked about kids, and after 10 years together it was feeling like we would move in that direction, so the timing was perfect.

It was a very exciting time, that pregnancy. Beth was intent on doing a drug-free, home birth with midwives, so we did our monthly check at the midwifery and made incredible friends with the midwives and their assistants. It was a beautiful process. We were such typical first-time parents: We played classical music through headphones on her belly; Beth was pristine in her diet; we did all the tests. At one point, one of the ultrasounds showed it was a boy! We named him Cole, in an inspired tribute to Brother Ni-col-as.

In January we took a trip to the Big Island in Hawaii. We went on magical adventures to the volcanoes, and even did some off-road Jeep riding. With a six-months-pregnant woman, maybe not the smartest thing I've done in life, but you don't know what you don't know.

The due date came and went. Finally, on Sunday, April 20, 2003, Beth started having contractions. At noon, we were doing some gardening in the back yard and Beth sat to rest. I put my hand on her belly and felt the baby kicking through the thin wall of skin. I thought, *What a wild and amazing sensation that is!*

The contractions became stronger through the day. By 6 p.m. they were coming more frequently, so we called the midwife, Amy, to come over. She and her team, Shawn and Lynn, arrived soon after. Beth's mom had been with us for a few weeks and we were all expectant. Oh, wait, it was Beth who was expecting. (Bad joke!) Anyway, I had made Beth a hot bath and she was in it when Amy came in. I was sitting next to her on the side of the tub.

Amy asked Beth, "How are you doing?"

Beth said, "Other than the pain?" We all laughed. She continued, "The contractions are coming more and more but I haven't felt the baby kick for a while, probably since early afternoon."

The silence. The look on Amy's face. Then she jumped into action, grabbing the fetal monitor (that little microphone used to hear the baby's heartbeat) and put it on Beth's big round belly. White noise where normally there was the rapid patter-patter of the baby's tiny heart. Amy said, "This isn't normal—we need to get to the hospital to check it out."

The calm but immediate rush, getting Beth out of the tub and dressed, grabbing a bag of things, getting into the cars, the silent ride to the hospital. We didn't know how not normal it was.

We got checked into the hospital room. It was, like most hospital rooms, sterile and white. Soon after we checked in, a young, just woke-up-from-a-nap technician came in to do an ultrasound. I'll never forget his *Oh man, another ultrasound for some hyper and pathetically over-worried parents* expression. I'll also never forget as, practically rolling his eyes, he put the device on her belly and the picture came on the screen—and nothing was moving. As he became more alert to the situation and almost became panicked when no heartbeat came and the baby didn't move. And how he looked around at us and said, "Oh my God, I'm so sorry."

I got to experience that. I got to be with my wife, her mom, and our three midwives as it sank in, there, at that hospital, that our Cole was dead. I got to experience being up all night, as Beth was still in labor and there was nothing to do but go through the birth process. At one point, Beth and I were alone and had been for several hours. I thought that our midwives, Amy, Shawn, and Lynn (we called them our three angels), had gone home. It was 2 a.m. and my attention was on how life is more precarious than we can ever imagine. But the angels came back (they had gone to a separate room to grieve), and we spent the early morning hours getting to know each other, talking about life (Amy had spent a couple of years in Japan), and speculating about what our baby would look like.

At 8:00 the next morning, with Beth still in labor, the hospital priest, black robes and all, came in. "Would you like me to do a blessing?" He looked grave and serious. Beth wasn't going to have anything to do with it.

Seeing her look, he asked instead if I would like to meet in his office. I'm all about spirituality and would have welcomed a chance to talk with any spiritually minded person then, so I went.

I followed him to his office and we sat. It was a sweet little room, pictures of Jesus and a crucifix on the wall. Simple. Ah, memories of my childhood. He smiled and asked about my religious background. I told him a short version of Sunday school, and how my beliefs had expanded to exploring all religions during my time in Japan.

He said, "If you accept Jesus into your life right now, your son will go to heaven."

I said, "Um, I think my son is going to heaven regardless of what I do."

The priest said, "We are all born sinners, including your son, and you must accept Jesus in order for him to go to heaven."

Are you fucking kidding me? I thought. *You're telling me my dead child who's about to be born will go to hell if I don't accept Jesus here on the spot?* But what I said was, "This is ridiculous, my son is pure and beautiful, and I hate that you are calling him a sinner. I'm outta here." And got up and left.

I saw him in the hall at some point later and I smiled. One bartending lesson I had learned, the one I'd applied to Sunamori so many years later, is that grudges get you nowhere—especially with a priest.

●●●●

I grew up a Lutheran, since that was the thing you did in my middle-class neighborhood in Columbus. Or else you were Catholic. There were a few Jews that I knew of, and other than the fact that they didn't celebrate Christmas (which I thought was a shame because they missed out on the presents), I didn't think much of it: whatever, let's go out and play. My parents didn't really believe in being a Lutheran in particular, but we went to church and Sunday school every week because that's what they did when they were kids, and on back through the ages. I was in the choir and we did the summer camps and other activities. It was actually pretty fun and I was with a great group of kids. There was some smoking and I'm sure a lot of sex between the teenage counselors, and I'm not sure how much they believed in Jesus either. I guess that's not the right way to say it—how can you not believe in Jesus? The real question is whether he is the one and only son of God—and if you don't believe that, you go to hell. I don't think they believed that. But I've said it before and I'll say it again, What the heck do I know? Who am I to judge? I get to be alive, experience all the beliefs in the world, and smile.

The thing is, I don't not believe in anything. That's not a typo. I don't *not* believe in anything. Really, it's all good. My friend Ghassan is Muslim. I've spent time with him in Dubai and visited him and his family in Amman, Jordan. Although he's a devout Muslim, he has nothing against my having been raised Christian, or that I now fluctuate between Buddhist and atheist. I like that about most of my friends: Christian, Jewish, Buddhist, Muslim, or noncommittal. In fact, I find most humans are like that: "You get to believe what you want, I get to believe what I want; now let's laugh and dance!"

Watching *Kung Fu* in the early '70s may have been the start of my spiritual evolution, but it was followed by an even more magical moment in July 1979. I was working part time for a candle manufacturers' rep company. We had a showroom in an industrial complex on the outskirts of Columbus that had dozens of glass displays of candles from 50 or so candle companies from around the country. Once a month for three days, retail buyers from the Columbus area would come place orders for candles to sell in their stores. I was making extra money as an assistant (those were the days of adding extra drums to my drum set), helping unpack boxes of candles and set up displays. There were glass candles, oil candles, candles covered in shells, and even a giant, five-foot-tall parrot candle. It's amazing what kind of shit you can put a flame on.

Anyway, one of the manufacturers was Carleen, a beautiful 28-year-old woman who had a company called Feather River Pottery. She produced oil-burning ceramic candles she hand-made at her shop in Chico, California. She came in town every few months to help out in the showroom and sell her candles. They were her candles, after all, so when a retail buyer stopped by her display, she could sell a ton. The buyers usually bought cases of candles from her for their stores.

Carleen was hip and cool. Although she was way out of my league (too hot and too old), we got high, drank wine, and talked a lot. I was 17 and loved the attention. She spoke a strange language. She used terms like karma, fate, astrology, astral projection, soul mates, meditation, and reincarnation. I didn't think much of it—she lived in California after all and was a bit kooky, but whatever, we had a great time hanging out.

One evening, dusting off shelves together and getting ready for the next day's show, I reached up to pull a big candle—five inches around, six inches tall, and very solid—off a high shelf. I had to hop to grab it and as I came down, my wrist hit the top edge of the shelf, flicking the bulky, heavy piece of wax backward out of my hand end over end—right into Carleen's face. She was standing in back of me and didn't see it coming. Blood squirted, she collapsed. It had hit her right between the eyes, splitting open a gash three inches long just above and between her eyebrows. "Oh my God!" I yelled and people working nearby came running. I stood in shock as the others attended to her. I just stood there saying, "I'm so sorry, I'm so sorry, I'm so sorry."

Carleen, dazed but conscious, blood soaking the paper towels now on her face, looked up at me through one of her quickly bruising eyes and said, "Ted, everything happens for a reason." And smiled. I swear to God, she smiled.

As they helped her up and rushed her to the hospital, I stood there with that swirling in my head: *Everything happens for a reason.* When I saw her the next day, I was sick over what I had done. This beautiful woman had 18 stitches across her forehead and her face was black and blue. She came up and hugged me and said again, "It all happens for a reason, Ted."

At that moment there was a crack in my consciousness. Not the whack on the side of the head that would come years later in Reno, but a crack. I knew at that moment there was more to the physical and mental suffering and the grabbing up of things that had been determining my life so far. It was a crack that, I believe, broke open while jogging years later at Osaka Castle.

Carleen and I remained good friends, and a few years later she told me to read Shirley McClaine's book *Out on a Limb*, an autobiography about her spiritual journey. I did, and my lifelong exploration of "what the fuck are we doing here anyway?" began in earnest. Whether soul mates exist or not is anyone's guess, but if they do, Carleen is one of mine.

What I've learned through the years is that most religious teachings talk about having a relationship with your "Creator" or "God." In alignment with that, I've come to believe the earth and everything on it, along with the sun, the planets, the trillions of galaxies, all of this we call life, is not "just here." It was created by, or better yet, is being created every moment by "something." Most people call that "something" God. To connect with this "thing," this Creator, this God, to have a relationship with "it" is, to me, a great purpose to live for. Most people, through the rituals of their religion, are doing just that; creating a relationship with their God. Meditation, prayer, counting beads, pilgrimages, all of it helping people get closer to God. Very cool. But for me the easiest way to have that relationship is to simply be fully alive in the present moment. Living. No rituals, no beliefs, no gurus, no have-to's, no thoughts on what this Creator might have in store for me when I die, or their intention for my life to be a certain way while I live. No judgments on anyone or anything. Just simply smile. Be present. And there I am, with God.

Practice

Think about your religion, the rituals you follow and beliefs that have been passed down from your family. Honoring those rituals and beliefs, set them aside for a moment and think about what God or the Creator, is. Enjoy those thoughts, then let them go for now.

Get To—Smile—Be with God.

Practice

Next time you see an infant, put your attention on them for a minute. Hold them if you can. Realize how special life is and that each human on the planet is a miracle.

Get To—Smile—Miracles!

34. Get To Cole Grace

*What the caterpillar calls the end of
the world, the master calls a butterfly.*
—*Richard Bach*, Illusions

I had put the incident with the well-meaning priest behind me.
I had more important things to think about, like Beth, who was
now in full labor.

I'm not going to try and be accurate with the accounts of
this or any labor. Only Beth and women who have given birth
could do that. But it was wild from my viewpoint. The angels
were there, and Beth's mom along with several nurses and the
doctor. Beth was a champion, and through her moaning and
pain, laughed and smiled. I love her for that. Finally, at 10:30
a.m. the most beautiful—precious—are you ready—LITTLE
GIRL was born. Not a boy. A girl. So much for ultrasounds
being effective in telling the sex of a child! And then, there we
were, with our little girl, whom we promptly renamed Cole
Grace to make it sound at least a little girly, holding her, crying,
laughing, grieving, while at the same time getting to appreciate
the incredible nature of life. It's so precious, tenuous, and special, and in those moments you wonder how we can take even
one second alive on the planet for granted. We each held her in
turn, knowing that would be the first and last snuggle we would
have. She was beautiful. We asked for a birth certificate but
were told since she didn't take a breath it was a stillbirth. In
other words, she wasn't "technically" born, meaning she
couldn't have one. What the hell? Who made that rule? We got

to experience those hours alone that day after allowing them to take her away, and then leaving the hospital the next morning with, as they say, empty arms. Cole Grace was sent to the crematorium.

A few days later, on a warm early Thursday morning, the three angels came over to check on us. We hugged, cried, laughed (lots of that over and over). We were huddled in a circle sitting on the floor in our living room, the sun was shining in and birds were chirping, and Beth said she wanted to play a song by Jane Siberry. It was called "Calling All Angels," and as it played we cried our eyes out, swaying and singing, "Calling all angels, calling all angels, walk me through this world, don't leave me alone." It was perfect.

Amy said, "What album is that from?"

Beth said, "I don't remember, I've had the CD forever." I got up and went to the CD player and grabbed the case. As I sat back down, reading the cover, I thought I was seeing things. The women were all looking at me, saying, "What's up?" I was silent.

"Come on," Lynn said, "what's the name of the album?"

I looked up slowly, not crying, but my eyes filled with tears of wonderment. I said, "The title of the album is *When I Was a Boy*."

The following Sunday, we had a service at our house to honor Cole Grace's birth and death. Honoring her path, as short as it was, through the birth/death life cycle that we all experience eventually.

There was no cause of death determined. If we had been doing a regular hospital birth, we would have left for the hospital about when Amy arrived, so that wouldn't have made any difference. Of course, I look at the Jeep ride in Hawaii as a potential cause. But the fact is, she just died. Dad died on his 75th birthday, was that too short? Mom was 78—was that okay? Nick was 38. Cole Grace had nine months! I've come to realize that I am not in a position to judge the right amount of time any one human should be alive on the planet. I just don't know.

Anyway, 50-plus people showed up and it was an amazing gathering of family and friends who hugged us and loved us. We got to experience love at levels I had only dreamed about. Talk about paying respects. It had a whole new meaning for me. Did I mention that we cried and laughed a lot?

● ● ● ●

After Cole Grace was born, we thought we'd better get some grief counseling, so we went to a group for bereaved parents. We showed up at a community center one night about 10 days after her birth and walked in, and there were 15 or so people sitting at a large round table. It was very somber. My heart was pounding. I held Beth's hand a little tighter and we looked at each other thinking, *We shouldn't be here.*

We sat, and then one by one, each person or couple told their story, of how many months or years earlier their children had died. One had been hit by a truck at 13. Another was mauled to death by a tiger when he was working as an assistant at a show in Las Vegas. It went on and on. We were in shock. We were new, so the last to go. When it was finally our turn, I said, "I really don't have anything to share. Our baby died at birth, but it's nothing compared to you guys. We have incredible compassion but we don't belong."

They said, "Oh, you're just in shock." They were right about that, we were shocked that there is a world of grief out there that we can't even imagine. We got to experience that—and when time for the next meeting rolled around, we decided not to go back.

There are two main things I've come to realize about grieving. First if there is a God, a Creator, or whatever you call it, who created this whole experience we're having, it's their way of making sure we absolutely appreciate life so we keep it going. Someone dies, there is grief, and grief sucks, so we do everything we can to stay alive. After those moments of grief we hopefully learn to be present to the miracle of the unfolding wildness of life. This is smart planning to keep the species propagating.

Grieving is selfish. That's not bad, but it is the truth. The more we grieve, the less we can feel gratitude for the experience we had with that being who has died, however long or short their life was. The more we grieve, the more we're not honoring the destiny of the soul (or whatever it is) that had its particular path through this life. Grieve hard, cry, scream, laugh hysterically, scream, and cry some more. Then smile. You'll be next, and the sooner you get back to living now, not in the past, the more fulfilled your world will be, and the more you'll fulfill what the world needs of you. We get to do this thing called life, grieving included.

Every day, whenever you can, remember to breathe deeply and repeat to yourself: *Get To—Smile—Life.*

Practice

Go to the place where a loved one is buried or memorialized. Sit quietly there. Cry for a bit if that feels right. Then laugh. Start with a chuckle if you need to. But laugh with the beauty of the life you have, and the life that they had.

Get To—Smile—Grieve.

"I FEEL THAT PERHAPS THIS TINY LITTLE SOUL

WAS NOT NEARLY AS TINY AS WE MIGHT IMAGINE

BUT ACTUALLY TIMELESS

HUGE AND WISE WELL BEYOND OUR IMAGINATION

AND MAYBE JUST MAYBE

TAKING THE FINAL SPIN ON HER KARMIC WHEEL

A SOUL SO PERFECT

SHE ONLY HAD ONE MORE THING TO EXPERIENCE

AND THAT SHE DID

AND WE GOT THE HONOR OF BEING HER PARENTS"

Email we sent to family and friends, April 2003.

35. Get To Have More Kids

What a day; hiking, taking it all on.
Loving the kids.
—*Journal entry, Costa Mesa,*
December 4, 2011

A month after Cole's service, I found a spot on my arm I wanted checked out. So I looked in the Yellow Pages for a dermatologist. Of the many practices, I found one with a Dr. Cole Fulwider. Well, that's an easy enough choice—Cole!—so I picked him. I made an appointment for a few weeks later, and Beth came with me. When we arrived, I filled out the forms sitting there in the waiting room and then gave them to the receptionist. She said, "Ok, have a seat, the doctor will be with you in a moment. She's just finishing up with another patient."

She. Dr. Cole Fulwider was a she.

We got to experience so many magical moments like that, feeling the joy and grief of Cole's life in waves. Then, a year later, Beth was pregnant again. This time, we went to a high-risk pregnancy doctor almost weekly to make sure everything was fine. This time, there was no doubt it was a boy. This time, on January 13, 2005, a beautiful boy we named Will was born in a kiddie pool in our bedroom. Surrounded by some very excited midwives!

Three years later, on March 5, 2008, at 6 a.m., Beth started having contractions with our third child. Again, every precaution taken, it clear that a baby girl was going to come forth, and we were so excited—well, *I* was excited. Beth was giving birth and was not quite so excited in that moment. I will say that I have more than the most incredible respect for Beth and her determination to have a natural birth. She's a hero! All women who give birth, in any way, are heroes.

At 8 a.m. I called the midwife, Jane, and said, "She's having contractions." Jane checked in with Beth and said, "Let me know when the contractions are closer."

At 9 a.m. I called again and said, "Okay, now you should really come over." Her famous last words were, "I'm on my way."

At 10 a.m., with Beth in full labor, I called her back. "Where the hell are you?"

"Ted," she said, "I'm stuck in traffic on the 405 freeway. I'm not going to make it. Put me on speaker; you're going to deliver."

What? But I took a deep breath, smiled, and thought, *Yep, I get to do this!*

Beth's mom (an incredible presence at each birth) was with us in the bedroom while our friend Trish comforted Will through "Mommy's moaning" in the living room. Another magical event was about to happen. Jane talked to Beth, who was kneeling beside the bed (she had decided against the kiddie pool this time), through each contraction. She was coaching me and telling me what to do. Really, my job was simply to support Beth. Soon the baby's head came out.

"She's not breathing!" I reported, as calmly as my racing heart would allow.

"That's okay, it's normal," Jane said. "One more push, Beth, you can do it."

She roared, and the baby came out into my hands, and she was as slippery as can be, and I dropped her. She fell (about 12 inches), hit the floor, and started crying. Trying not to panic, I calmly picked her up, untangled the umbilical cord from around Beth's leg, helped her to sit on the edge of the bed, and handed her the beautiful, crying human being.

I sat next to her and put my arm around her, and that's how the midwives found us when they burst into the room five minutes later. All in scrubs, they took over—we were in good hands. Our little Nia was born. What a Get To experience. Just as life was so precarious with Cole Grace, I realized life was so resilient with Nia. Life wants to be born, and to live.

Practice

Next time you're with a child somewhere between the ages of 3 and 12, sit with your attention fully on them. No matter what they are doing, know they are perfect just as they are. Remember they were born and are going to die, like all of us, and they are getting to do this thing called life.

Get To—Smile—Be with kids.

Will only seconds old. In the baby pool in our bedroom, January 2005.

36. Get To Be Happy

I have realized that my thoughts are useless. They are not me. Now I realize that other people's thoughts are useless. I don't need to care what they think! I am free to be me.
—*Journal entry, Osaka, Japan, March 20, 1992*

The journey of one's life doesn't end until you take your last breath. And I suppose if you believe in reincarnation, not even then. For me, I'm still breathing. In 2006 I got caught up in the real-estate fervor that swept the country and, using money from our personal home equity, bought eight rental houses across the country. I hung on as the economy crashed in 2008, but I got to experience foreclosure on all of them by 2010. In March 2011, along with two other ex-Sunamori employees, I started Blue Sky International, another licensing company in Tokyo, this time representing MGM Studios, CBS, and Jack Nicklaus. But after the earthquake and subsequent tsunami in northern Japan that same month, the economy went stagnant, and by the end of 2013 we were running out of money. One less employee to pay, me, was a great solution to help the company survive, so when I was offered a job at DHX Media's licensing arm CPLG in Holly-wood, I handed the reins to my partners in Tokyo. The rising sun of Japan had set for me, at least for now.

Through it all, sometimes I've laughed until I cried, and cried until I laughed. But here's what I've come to know: the decision to be happy, regardless of all outside circumstances, can be a spiritual journey and is probably one of the most important choices you can make. There is suffering in the world—acknowledged. There is heartache, pain, cruelty, and injustice—I got it. We are going to die—yep. I know it's a lot to ask a human to be happy in spite of it all. But when we are free of physical and mental suffering, I feel it is our duty to be happy—*because we get to*. Of course, there's really no duty. It's a choice. But it sure would be nice if people who can do so choose to be happy.

I don't know about you, but when I'm feeling crummy, being with a happy child makes me smile. Being with happy *people* makes me smile. If you can be happy, why not be so and spread that to others. Why not bring that to the world if you are able to? Only you can judge if you have too much physical or mental suffering to be happy, but although there may be some discomfort in either, please consider a happy thought and find the momentum in that. Really, just be happy. In the midst of it all, after a good cry maybe, or while eating a toasted peanut-butter-and-jelly sandwich, remember where you are in this vast universe, and smile. And pass it on. It's a beautiful thing.

Practice

Are you ready? Say it with me:

Get To—Smile—Be Happy!

Epilogue

I've been writing this for over a year but it seems like I wrote the introduction ages ago, almost like a distant dream. But here we are. I got to do this (write), and you, fellow human, got to do that (read). And just as the front and back of a coin cannot be separated, the writing and reading of this book cannot be separated. It is a single event that we participated in together. I am grateful and thankful beyond measure for your joining me.

Have you done the exercises? Have you had a shift in attitude? Have you tasted the ginger in the almond butter?

For me, writing this has been a journey in itself. Finding the quotes at the beginning of each chapter, and creating (and doing) the exercises at the end of each chapter, have allowed me to go even deeper into the Get To Principle. I had lived a Get To life before starting—I'm now fully immersed in it. I'm happier and more content. My relationships with my family and friends have deepened. I smile a lot, and when I don't, when I feel worried or pissed off, I get to feel that. And realizing I get to do that, I start to smile, and soon enough I'm back to feeling at ease with the world.

My hope is that by being part of my journey, through reading about it, you are feeling the same. And I hope you will continue to use the *Get To Principle* and apply the *Get To—Smile—Do it!* mantra in your day-to-day life. To that end, I would like to offer a place to go for support: **www.gettobehappy. com**. Here you'll find resources to help you stay engaged with the Get To Principle. There's no selling. Okay, just a little selling—but who doesn't want a Get To bracelet to put on their wrist to remind them to *Get To—Smile—Do it?* And maybe some organic almond butter with ginger pieces in it. But really it's just a place for support for your Get To journey.

I'll end with my favorite quote. Remember it from the beginning of the book?

You're born, and then you die. And in between you Get To do this thing called life!

Each word you read is life unfolding in front of you. Each inhale, each exhale, each moment, you get to have. I hope you feel more engaged with the experience you are having, more alive. I hope my journey has inspired your journey as a human on the planet.

With appreciation and love,

Ted

August 17, 2017

Acknowledgements

Over the years I've read hundreds of acknowledgements in the books I've picked up. Or rather, I've started to read the acknowledgements . . . and then stopped. First I'd think, *Who the hell are all these people the author is acknowledging?* And, *Why should I care about reading about them?* I thought, *Yeah, if I ever write a book I'll just skip writing the acknowledgement page, or if I do, I'll stick it in the back.*

But here I am, ready to go to print, realizing there are many people I'd like to acknowledge. Uh-oh. Another case of judging the shit out of something I have no idea about. I'll still leave it here in the back of the book, but its importance is strong in my heart. You can, like me, stop reading this, because—well, because I'm going to acknowledge people, starting with Mr. Kowolsky, my seventh-grade band teacher. He suggested that I sucked so bad at the trumpet I should maybe do something easier, like banging things with sticks, which led to my liking to play drums, which led to my $500 million Pepsi deal. Too much of a stretch? Hmm . . .

Let's get to present day and make the acknowledging part of this book short and sweet. Short so you can move on in life, and sweet, because really, without the people mentioned here, there is no way you'd be holding this book in your hands. I wrote some words, but a team of people brought it to life.

For everyone mentioned in the book my thanks couldn't be stronger for your being in my life.

And those not mentioned in the book:

Dave Brown, a sage, a great friend, and a mentor in life. You've got the Cup of Life.

John Catalina and Andrew Silberman, life and business coaches who, each in his own way, slapped me numerous times, saying, "Are you kidding me? You think you can do this alone?" I love you guys.

John Davidson, my right-hand man in the Get To Journey. He keeps saying, "Ted, this is fucking awesome, man." Thank you for your wisdom, wingman.

Rose Porterfield and Henry Unger. They are just friends. But now that you know how much acknowledgements have come to mean to me, the fact that they are here means the word "friends" doesn't come close to describing our bond.

Tony Frescura, whom I met in San Diego more than 30 years ago. Although I hadn't seen him in many, many years, he recently invited me to his daughter's wedding. Two-hundred-plus people. I arrived and looked for my name card at one of the many round tables near the back of the room. He came up, hugged me, and said, "What are you doing back here? You're sitting next to my Dad at the head table." I cried. Feeling the word "friend" is more powerful than the sound it makes when it comes out of your mouth.

I love the Yiddish word *bashert*. For you fellow non-Jews it means something like "meant to be" or "everything happens for a reason." But those words don't quite get it, and unless you have a great Jewish friend like Harriet Cook to teach you the deeper meaning, you're out of luck.

Seven years ago, at a business seminar in a Los Angeles Airport hotel ballroom, the speaker, T. Harv Eker, said from the stage to the several hundred attendees, "Get an accountability partner." *What the hell is that?* I thought. Whatever it meant, I was hyped up from Harv's presentation, so I turned to my friend Jill Morris, who was standing next to me, and said, "Wanna give it a try?" Every Monday since that day, for the last seven years, without fail, I send an e-mail to Jill listing the things I plan to do that week. She does the same. On the following Sunday, without fail, I write an email detailing what I did, or didn't do. She does the same. For seven years. I say "without fail," but to be fair, there have been a handful of Tuesdays when I've gotten an email from Jill saying, "Where the hell are your goals?" I get them to her soon after. She's tough, but that's what you want in an accountability partner. Through this process we have created miracles in our respective lives.

Six months after beginning writing, I didn't know if I was anywhere near on track with a readable book. I'd never done this before (I'm not counting *The Babysitters Business Guide*, which was a much less ambitious project). I needed help, and my good friend Andrew Lombardi (dude, that's an acknowledgement) introduced me to Phil Dunn. For a few bucks Phil said he'd read and advise. We spent Saturday mornings together for several months. Among other things, he suggested adding exercises at the end of the chapters. He wins the idea prize.

I mentioned Andrew above, but that didn't really express how grateful I am for his friendship and sharing his Internet savvy. I was about to send a Western Union telegram announcing the book release and he suggested I use Instagram and Twitter. Boy, was that close!

Thirty years ago I met a guy handling publishing deals for James Dean books. John Appuhn. I remembered him as being a nice guy. I found him on Facebook and said, "Hey buddy, long time no talk. I need someone to edit my book for spelling and grammar and book design. Do you know anyone?" For the editing he introduced me to Diana Plattner.

In one of her first emails to me, Diana told me a parable: *An author and an editor were lost in the desert and on the verge of death. They came upon an oasis and stumbled to the pool of water. The author, lips cracked, barely able to speak, falls on his knees and scoops a handful of water into his mouth. Then he hears a tinkling sound and looks over to see the editor pissing in the water. Incredulous, the author squeaks out in a dying whisper, "What—are—you—doing?" The editor says, "Making it better."* Diana took my baby, my manuscript that I was so proud of, and pissed all over it. Pages and pages of edits that took months and months to work on. It was a magical process and I love her for it—and hope I never get lost in the desert with her.

John's other introduction, Bob Cashatt, is a master at book design and made this look better than I ever could have imagined. Thank you both!

The original subtitle was "One Man's Journey Through Life." Gag me. Kaia Alexander suggested "Stories and Secrets to Loving the Sh*t Out of Life." She said something like, "Ted, this is no feel-good, get-happy book. This is raw life, and you happily drop the F-bomb throughout. Let people know what they're in for." Kaia has been a most perfect guide.

Some readers of the early drafts who gave invaluable feedback are Terry, Abdallah, Jamie, Dottie, Matt, Patrik, Aleks, Theresa, Masen, Steve, Sheila, Charles, Sanae, Kirsti (sort of), Claudia, and Jo: I am indebted to each one of you, and many others.

To everyone at Upper Arlington High School in the late '70s—the jocks, the bandies, the druggies, the preps, the nerds, and everyone else without a label—thanks for being the framework of my life! Deno, Tim, David, and Craig, among many others, were awesome friends.

I have been inspired by Farah Merhi, creator of Inspire Me! Home Decor, and honored to call her our client. I'm even more honored to call her my friend. Along with my colleague Erin Dippold, watching Farah shine on QVC was magical.

There are hundreds of people who influenced me over my business career, especially my community of licensing-industry colleagues and friends. I'm proud to be with them as part of the Licensing Industry Merchandise Association (LIMA). To every one of you, thank you.

There have also been thousands of people I've crossed paths with, if only momentarily, who influenced my life without even knowing it. Allow me to give you an example:

In 2005, I was in the Singapore Airlines lounge at LAX waiting for a flight to Japan. I'm a Delta guy but Singapore was offering a good business-class upgrade deal so I took it. Other than me and a young woman (from Singapore?) behind a desk at the door, the "premier lounge" was empty.

Not long after I had settled in, a burly-looking guy came in and sat in the corner. Weird. A few minutes later another guy and some young gal came in. They sat 20 feet away and started talking about a movie called *Kingdom of Heaven*. Then it hit me; Orlando Bloom. He was attending his movie premier in Tokyo. She was obviously his assistant. I got up and walked out of the lounge to call Kathy and tell her.

The burly guy followed me out. *Oh*, I realized, *body guard*. Making sure I'm not paparazzi. "Hi Kath. I'm here at LAX and just wanted to say hi before I head to Japan. I wanted to tell you about Dad and say how great he looked the other day." I chatted about some other BS for a bit. The burly guy, satisfied, went back in the lounge.

"Oh my God, Orlando Bloom is sitting in the lounge with me," I finally whispered.

Kathy said, "Well, go up and say hi, what's the matter with you? You always meet people."

"I don't know, I just feel weird—but okay, I'll do it," I said, and went back in the lounge.

I sat in my seat as I thought of the right approach. They called the flight. *Shit*. Orlando and girl got up and went out. I followed. I could feel the burly guy come out after me. I figured I'd say something to Orlando at the gate. He got into the first-class line. No one else was in it. Shit. I got in the business-class line but was behind three people. I'd lost my chance. I walked on to the almost-empty flight and, 11 hours later, we landed in Tokyo.

We deplaned and I followed a little behind him. He turned and looked at me, I stopped and we locked eyes. *You dick, you've been wanting to say something to me since Los Angeles and now's your chance*, his eyes said. I wondered if I was gay because I thought he was beautiful and my heart pounded. I didn't say anything. He turned and walked toward immigration. I spent the next several months analyzing myself on whether I'm gay and on why I didn't engage Orlando Bloom in some sort of conversation. On the first count, after 55 years on the planet, I'm pretty sure I'm not, and on the second count, I never figured it out. Who knows why I didn't talk to him, and does it really matter? The point is I got to experience that. Thanks, buddy!

Another time, there was a woman behind the counter at 7-11 . . .

Lastly, I want to thank life. You are a gift for me and I intend to honor you, as often as I can, by being happy and sharing that with the world.

About the Author

Ted Larkins is an accomplished business executive and entrepreneur with a focus on international licensing. Ted co-developed a leading entertainment licensing company in Tokyo, representing major movie studios that included Paramount Pictures, Sony Pictures, and 20th Century Fox. He's worked on projects with Jon Bon Jovi, Jack Nicklaus, Mariah Carey, and many other artists. He is on the board of directors of the Licensing Industry Merchandise Association (LIMA), co-chairing the charity committee and sitting on the executive committee. He is a guest lecturer for the UCLAx Entertainment Studies and Performing Arts program.

He wrote this book over a year-and-a-half period from 2016 to 2017, during his daily four-hour train commute to work in Hollywood. Ted lives with his wife of 22 years and their two children in Southern California.

Lightning Source UK Ltd.
Milton Keynes UK
UKHW02f0218140818
327177UK00027BA/1647/P